BREAKTHROUGH!

BREAKTHROUGH!

A 7-Step System for Developing
Unexpected and Profitable Ideas

PAUL KURNIT AND STEVE LANCE

AMACOM AMERICAN MANAGEMENT ASSOCIATION

New York • Atlanta • Brussels • Chicago • Mexico City • San Francisco
Shanghai • Tokyo • Toronto • Washington, D. C.

This publication is designed to provide accurate and authoritative information in regard to the subject matter covered. It is sold with the understanding that the publisher is not engaged in rendering legal, accounting, or other professional service. If legal advice or other expert assistance is required, the services of a competent professional person should be sought.

Library of Congress Cataloging-in-Publication Data

Kurnit, Paul.
Breakthrough! a 7-step system for developing unexpected and profitable ideas / Paul Kurnit and Steve Lance.
    p. cm.
Includes bibliographical references and index.
ISBN-13: 978-0-8144-1562-7
ISBN-10: 0-8144-1562-8
1. Creative ability in business. 2. Success in business. 3. Marketing—Management. I. Lance, Steve. II. Title. III. Title: Seven step system for developing.
HD53.K867 2011
658.4'01—dc22

2010018683

About AMA
American Management Association (www.amanet.org) is a world leader in talent development, advancing the skills of individuals to drive business success. Our mission is to support the goals of individuals and organizations through a complete range of products and services, including classroom and virtual seminars, webcasts, webinars, podcasts, conferences, corporate and government solutions, business books and research. AMA's approach to improving performance combines experiential learning—learning through doing—with opportunities for ongoing professional growth at every step of one's career journey.

Printing number
10 9 8 7 6 5 4 3 2 1

To Susan, my biggest breakthrough was marrying you and creating our biggest ideas:
Ara, Jesse, Eric, Hannah, Juliet, and Oliver

—Paul Kurnit

To my sons, Max and Daniel, who continue to inspire me in ways I never imagined.

—Steve Lance

CONTENTS

INTRODUCTION

What's the Big Idea?

Not just THE Big Idea. What's YOUR Big Idea?

Is your company creating breakthrough, winning products and services within your industry? Is the pursuit of Big Ideas standard operating procedure for your business? Why does it always seem that *other* companies develop new ideas, products, and services while you continue to struggle to hold onto your existing share of the market? Why aren't you able to cultivate big, new ideas, let alone move your good idea to the next step? Why aren't you taking steps to make your company the next Apple or Google or Starbucks or Dell or Lite Beer—even Chia Pet or any other one of the hundreds of global phenomena?

Yeah? We're waiting . . .

When was the last time you or your company came up with a breakthrough idea, product, or service? Never? Wait—never say *never*. We all come up with good ideas all the time. But it's not just about coming up with great ideas; it's about coming up with terrific ideas that actually make it to market. So how come your good ideas don't make it to market? And if they did, how come they didn't succeed? Why aren't you occupying the corner office at your company? Why aren't you rich, retired, and living *la vida loca* in Costa Rica?

Okay, fair enough, we're being a bit tough on you—and we're getting ahead of ourselves. Since this is our book and you're still reading, let's give you what we believe is the right answer: *It's so difficult at our company. There are so many impediments to getting at and launching Big Ideas.* Yes, that's YOUR right answer. And it's so easy to remain complacent and paralyzed beneath that answer. But the REAL right answer is, "You don't know there are steps you have to take."

People think breakthrough ideas are a matter of luck. The truth is, they're the result of careful thinking, planning, and execution. Smart steps can take a great idea and drive a brilliant result (yes, with a manageable dose of luck thrown into the mix). But without managing the smart steps there's virtually no chance that you'll land on, let alone launch, a Big Idea.

So what's your plan for making the seemingly impossible, possible?

Look around you. Every year, even in the worst of times, companies and individuals come to market with extraordinarily fresh, successful ideas. One thing that many of the best Big Ideas tend to have in common is that virtually everyone said the idea made no sense when they first heard it. There's no way it could ever succeed.

- *Starbucks.* Coffee at $3 a cup? Who would spend so much for a dollar cup of joe?

- *Perdue.* Turn chicken into a brand name? Ridiculous. Who needs a brand of chicken?

- *G.I. Joe.* Dolls for boys? Absurd. Boys don't play with dolls.

- *Google.* A search engine? Who needs a new search engine when you've got Netscape and Internet Explorer?

- *JetBlue.* Who needs another low-cost airline? Especially to Florida?

- *Twitter.* We have instant messaging and texting. We already have blogging. Who's going to micro-blog in 140-character messages?

Do you think they were all just lucky? Well, what about companies that got it wrong the first time but didn't give up?

- *Procter & Gamble.* They invented disposable diapers. But they had to relaunch Pampers multiple times before they found the winning message and created an entirely new product category.

- *Pringles.* Same story. An initial failure as a "stacked-chips-in-a-can" product. A success as a convenient, flavorful alternative to "greasy, regular chips."

- *E*TRADE.* A backroom processing application. Until their chairman was smart enough to see that the digital revolution meant the company could go directly to consumers and create a new industry called "online trading."

They all seem like good ideas—in retrospect. But how did they get to the marketplace? Because someone believed in them. Someone initially said, "This is a good idea." (No matter what everybody else may have said at first.)

Is that all you need?

If only . . .

If saying "This is a good idea" was all it took, then everyone would be an inventor with a multimillion-dollar idea to his or her credit. You need something more than just the good idea. You need the guts and conviction to bring the idea to life, and you need the intelligence and stick-to-itiveness to fulfill the following key statements:

"We can make this."

"We can make it happen."

"We can figure out the audience and the message."

"We can commit resources, time, and energy to do it."

In other words, you need a plan.

You with us so far? Good. Now, for the hard part. Without even knowing your company, product, or service, we'll guarantee that you don't know what the steps are to uncover and launch your Big Idea. Why can we make that claim? Because if you did know how to do it, you'd have been a huge success by now and we'd have read your story in *BusinessWeek, Forbes, Fortune,* and online.wsj.com.

Ouch. Yeah, that hurts. But we're trying to make a point. Which is that winning ideas aren't just the brainstorm of inspiration; they are the result of a methodical, step-by-step process of development, refinement, targeting, marketing, and market-place execution.

Miss any of the steps or get any of the steps wrong and you're doomed to failure. Get 'em all right and there's still a chance the market won't be ready for you. Bottom line: it's a crapshoot. But you can improve the odds tremendously in your favor by putting together a structured process. In other words, it might be a crapshoot, but with some smart planning you can be the house.

That's what *Breakthrough! A 7-Step System for Developing Unexpected and Profitable Ideas* is about. It outlines a step-by-step method for bringing Big Ideas, new products, or services to market.

Over the years, we've watched and participated in the launch of many successful products and services. We've also watched, and like many of you (we're humbled to admit), participated in the launch of a few huge failures.

We've come to understand the kind of vision and commitment it takes to get good ideas right and great ideas to market. Along the way we've seen and participated in the combination of delicious ingredients that lead to tasty success.

Breakthrough! is the distillation of all those winning steps. They're steps you can take no matter what your situation:

- You're the CEO of a major corporation and want to revitalize the company and its products or services.

- You're a brand manager at a packaged-goods company and want to extend your brand to take advantage of changes in consumer attitudes or shifts in your market.

- You're the sales director of a mid-sized firm and realize you're getting feedback from your existing customers (and companies that won't return your phone calls) that your offerings may no longer match the marketplace.

- You're a smart programmer with a tremendous knowledge of the Web but haven't hit on your Killer App yet.

- You're a small business in any size town or market any place in the world and realize you have to compete globally—no matter how big or how small you're perceived to be.

- You're a small office/home office (SOHO), one-person operation and need to separate yourself from countless other SOHO vendors in your field.

- You're in a service-related business and want to find the new feature or offering that will make your service invaluable to current and future customers.

In short, no matter who you are or what business you're in, you're going to have to start thinking about new products and services—and reading this book will be your first step toward breakthrough success.

When you read the topic headings of the seven steps, you'll say to yourself, "That's all I have to do?" And when you read the detailed description of each step, you'll groan to yourself, "I have to do all that?" It ain't easy, but it's doable. There are no shortcuts. You're going to have to get your organization in alignment and you're going to have to overcome a lot of inertia and resistance. Some of the inertia will be yours; the rest of the resistance will be systemic: a lot of people around you will resist following your lead and following these steps. But if you succeed, the rewards can be huge. Especially in the area of personal satisfaction, not to mention the staggering financial return. So actually, there is a shortcut. This book is dedicated to it. Get the steps right and you'll save huge amounts of time, energy, and money in bringing your Big Idea to the marketplace.

Give it a go. Take on the challenge of bringing your Big Ideas for your products and services to life. And as you bask in the light of your shining victory, please think of us and give a shout-out to this book.

ACKNOWLEDGMENTS

Paul Kurnit

Special thanks to our executive editor, Ellen Kadin, who instantly recognized the big idea of this book and championed it at every step. To Mike Sivilli, who had the big idea of putting us together with Carole Berglie, our copy editor, who "got" the book instantly and edited it in our voice and style. To Cathleen Ouderkirk, who dazzled us with a cover design that instantly captures the concept of the book. To Barry Richardson, Jenny Wesselmann, William Helms, and the team at AMACOM Books, who managed all the elements of this publishing enterprise so seamlessly. And, to Peter Hurley, whose headshots make us look better than anyone might think possible.

To Tom Griffin and Joe Bacal, my partners at Griffin Bacal, who approached every marketing, advertising, and entertainment initiative as if it were going to be the next Breakthrough—which they often became. To Steve Schwartz, head of marketing at Hasbro, who was our indispensible partner in the many

Breakthroughs we brought to the marketplace. To all the Griffin Bacal and Hasbro people who contributed mightily to the Breakthrough journey that was fundamental to the way we worked. To all my other marketing and advertising mentors, partners, colleagues, clients, and collaborators from the days at Benton & Bowles, Ogilvy & Mather, Pace University, and today in our work at PS Insights.

To my father and mother, Shep and Jean, whose life force always focused on Big Ideas in design, advertising, politics, and people. To my wife Susan and my kids, Ara and Jesse, who constantly inspire me as they approach their careers, everyday lives, and parenting through the lens of innovation. To my brothers, Rick and Scott, whose numerous big ideas and Breakthroughs make people's lives richer.

But most of all, to my coauthor, Steve Lance, who makes the writing fun and easy, who completes my sentences (and always makes them better), and who truly demonstrates how 1+1=3. On to the next book, Steve.

Steve Lance

Many thanks to our executive editor, Ellen Kadin, for being tough, focused, and on-message. To our copy editor, Carole Berglie, who caught every mistake—especially the ones we didn't know we made. To Cathleen Ouderkirk, who chose a cover design that catches everyone's eye. To Mike Sivilli, Barry Richardson, Jenny Wesselmann, William Helms, and all the team at AMACOM Books, who make our words turn into something real, tangible, and marketable.

To Christos Cotsakos and Jeff Woll, without whom I wouldn't be in the book-writing business. And of course to

Roger Feldman, without whom I'd probably be selling furniture somewhere in Connecticut.

To Norman Siegel, who still keeps a jaundiced eye on the whole enterprise—and keeps us on the straight and narrow.

To Doug Olney and Jeremy Berger, who keep giving us lessons in how to produce it smart, affordable, and good.

To Danielle Cacnio, our Web wunderkind, who makes sure we have a strong digital presence.

To Laura Masse and her contributions to the entire PS Insights enterprise.

To my brother, Paul Lance, the patriarch of the family writers (and there are more of us each year).

To all our interns. I hope they've learned as much from us and we've learned from them.

And especially to my coauthor, Paul Kurnit, who continues to display an unfailing optimism, a glorious sense of humor, and a shared cultural vernacular that makes working with him just an effortless delight. Here's to many more!

BREAKTHROUGH!

OVERVIEW:
What's a Big Idea?

A BIG IDEA is anything that can build new audiences, new customers, and new sales by mining undiscovered territory. It can be a brand-new product or service, a line extension, a related product—in fact, it can be just about anything. The only thing every breakthrough idea has in common is that after it's come to the marketplace, everyone else turns into Homer Simpson and says, "D'oh!"

What they mean is "Dough!" As in, "That's gonna make those people a *ton of money*. How come we didn't think of that?" Because to come up with a breakthrough idea, product, or service you've got to break out of the box of your existing marketplace thinking. And that's very hard to do. But, there are companies out there that are doing it all the time.

Arm & Hammer Baking Soda. This one is classic. Perhaps the granddaddy of all Big Ideas. *Conventional wisdom:* You should always have a box in your cupboard for baking. You use one or two tablespoons at a time. The package lasts forever— or close to it. After all, it's baking soda, right? *Big Idea:* Take the entire box and put it in the refrigerator to freshen things up. And when it stops working, pour it down the drain to freshen your sink.

Wow! That's three different Big Ideas in one. First, Arm & Hammer finds a new use for the product (a use customers were already doing; the manufacturer found out about it by conducting focus groups) to increase sales. Second, the manufacturer promoted the idea by suggesting you put the whole box in the refrigerator (you only need a few tablespoons in a dish, which you can change every few weeks). And third, they suggested pouring the box—80 percent of which was still good—down the drain to "freshen your drains." (Did you know you had a stale drain problem? We sure didn't!) Sales of Arm & Hammer Baking Soda took a quantum leap—it was a brilliant paradigm buster that jump-started sales of a sleepy staple.

Diet Coke/Coke Zero. *Conventional Wisdom:* Coca-Cola is the big gun of full-flavored cola beverages. Your brand is your brand; don't mess with the golden goose. *Big Idea:* Why try to build brand loyalty for a product no one's heard of (Tab) when you can leverage the mother-lode name into an arena people want—the Coke experience without the calories? So Diet Coke is born. And if men don't like the idea of drinking a "diet" cola, let's just call it Coke Zero and invite that Coke audience to the party with a brand they can call their own. Sometimes busting a paradigm doesn't involve reinventing your entire marketing and manufacturing approach. It just takes the courage to smartly extend it!

Lite Beer from Miller. Conventional wisdom: Guys drink beer for taste and to get drunk. They're proud of their beer-drinking ways and the number of brews they can put away in a sitting. You can't promote light beer as a dietary drink for men. They're not interested in admitting they're counting calories. *Big Idea:* "Less filling" means you can drink more. It's permission to beer binge without feeling full or uncomfortable. Beyond that, women would drink more beer if it weren't so fattening. Suddenly, brewers had the opportunity to significantly increase the size of their market. The danger here is in the marketing execution: You can't promote light beer as a drink for women; they're a secondary target. So the first attempts to market "light" beer were a disaster (read the case study on Gablinger's Beer) because they missed the marketing target (and it tasted awful). But when Miller Brewing Company started using ex-jocks to promote the "less filling/tastes great" concept, they suddenly had a winner—a big winner that opened a new category in the beer business: light (or Lite) beer.

By the way, later we'll talk more about understanding the difference between a failed idea and a failed marketing strategy. Some ideas are just plain bad. Others are good, but they take some effort to find the winning message. That was the case with Pampers. Procter & Gamble knew moms wanted the ease, convenience, cost savings, and less-mess approach of disposable diapers, but P&G couldn't find the winning message in launching the product. None of those points—points moms themselves raised in focus groups and consumer studies—resonated with the audience when P&G took Pampers to market. It wasn't until they hit on the strategy "keeps your baby drier" that sales took off. Because the real value to new moms in disposable diapers is what the diapers mean to their babies. And, yes, consumers lie in research all the time.

iPhone/iPhone Apps. Conventional Wisdom: Cell phones are about the convenience of being able to talk to friends on the go. They're the necessary hardware part of the telephone network's strategy to sell "minutes." *Big Idea:* The cell phone is just one function of the personal digital assistant, and if you open your architecture, you can create unprecedented demand from consumers for a new type of personal device. In fact, as of this writing, the Apple Store has sold more than a billion downloads of almost 50,000 different apps for the iPhone. Prior to the "open architecture" approach of Apple, this was a nonexistent business.

UPS. Conventional wisdom: United Parcel Service was in the business of package delivery. It was mostly a B-to-B operation. Stores would send merchandise to customers via their brown trucks. But customers had virtually no access to the service. *Big Idea:* With the acquisition of Mail Boxes, Etc. and a UPS rebranding effort, UPS has become an active—and friendlier— competitor to the U.S. Postal Service. Consumers go to UPS Stores in droves to mail their packages. And UPS delivery guys are friends to local merchants and residents alike as they make their way through numerous communities. "What can brown do for you?"

Big companies and big honking ideas, right? Well, Big Ideas aren't restricted to big companies or big product ideas. They also come from independents, entrepreneurs, and small businesses.

Animus Rex. A world-class Web design firm—in a very crowded field. Their first Big Idea was to create a Web management tool called EsKort that both increased client loyalty to them and their services and also gave clients the independence to manage their own Web sites. A win-win for Animus Rex and their clients. Their next Big Idea was to solve the needs of a specific industry—law firms. Law firms were moving to online digital platforms but had huge amounts of data to store. Animus Rex started specializing in law-firm Web design *and* data management, providing firms with an easy way to store and manage literally millions of pages of data.

Spam. That's right, spam. Not the food product made by Hormel Foods (although they probably could use a breakout idea or two), but the stuff you try not to get every day on your computer. *Conventional wisdom:* You cold-call via phone or by walking door-to-door. *Big Idea:* Use the new medium of digital communication to reach out to potential customers. A guy named Gary Turk claims to be the father of spam in a story he gave to National Public Radio in May 2008, commemorating the 30th anniversary of the first spam e-mail. According to Turk, in 1978 there were approximately 2,600 people on Arpanet (the predecessor to the Internet) and their e-mail addresses were listed in the directory. Turk sent unsolicited e-mails to 400 people on the list (more than 15 percent of the entire Internet at the time) and started an entirely new form of

annoying marketing. (Hey, we never said that all the breakthrough ideas would be loved by the rest of the world. It
worked for him at the time and that's all that counts.)

Scott Gutterson. A New York City–based tax attorney.
Scott realized that his client base was getting older—all his
clients were over 40. He also recognized that whenever he got
a new client it was because the person had gotten into financial
trouble chasing "a good idea." Scott felt it would be beneficial
to all his clients if he could address those common pitfalls
before people lost their money. The result was a new Web site
devoted to providing financial advice for young adults,
www.18-34 YoYoNow.com (You're On Your Own Now). It's
become a high-traffic site and a great new-business tool for a
new generation of clients.

. . .

WE CAN GO ON. In fact, throughout this book we'll talk
about products and services that landed on Big Ideas. You get
our point. Chances are, there are half a dozen possible game-
changing ideas within your own company's area of expertise
that can revolutionize or revitalize sales for your business.
They're there. They're lying beneath the surface of what you
already do well. You just need the commitment and the method
to mine them.

So what are you waiting for? As the Texas political commen-
tator Jim Hightower once observed, "There's nothing in the
middle of the road but a yellow line and dead armadillos." If you
play it safe, if you don't grow, you'll just disappear—merged
into a larger company or marginalized into irrelevance.

Companies need new ideas the way people need food. It's the energy that grows and sustains them. But where do they come from? Many people think breakthrough ideas are a matter of luck. But we'll show you how they are the result of careful planning, thinking, and execution.

When it comes to conceiving and launching Big Ideas, there are no guarantees—but follow our 7 steps to developing a block-buster phenomenon and you'll greatly improve your odds.

7 Steps Quick Start (Wallet Guide)

1. Put an end to business as usual.

2. Get business buy-in.

3. Organize the team and process.

4. Land on the big idea.

5. Build momentum for the idea.

6. Develop the plan.

7. Launch the idea.

We'll take you through these steps, one by one, to help you build your rule-breaking team and process. Along the way we'll answer the questions of how you create a big new idea; what qualifies as a standout product or service; how you develop marketing and marketing communication that surrounds the consumer; how you build a team to help get you there; who the partners are and what events are that will help drive the idea; and what the time frame is that will enable an idea to develop into a phenomenon.

When we're done, you'll know the secrets to success. Then all you have to do is get the buy-in (Step 2) and put together your winning team (Step 3). Then you'll be on your way.

So what are you waiting for? Let's get going!

STEP ONE

Put an End to
Business as Usual

How Ya Doin'?

THERE'S AN OLD show-business joke about a producer who opens a musical out of town. Opening night in Omaha, the show does $750 in ticket sales. A friend calls him up and says, "How'd the show go?" The producer answers, "Great! We sold $900 worth of tickets."

Besides lying about your results, which the Securities Exchange Commission, your investors, and your mother tend to frown upon, the question of how you're doing is one of the most difficult tasks a person has to do. It's also one of the most feared questions people in business hear all the time. Putting aside the lies, the fears, and the unwillingness to take the question seriously, take a moment to ask yourself what your answer would be.

It should be easy. After all, you've got only four choices: "Terrible"; "Could be better"; "Same old, same old"; and "Great, couldn't be better."

"Terrible." If your business isn't what it could be or isn't what it used to be, what are you doing about it? Most companies (especially small businesses) cling to the old rituals: cut their overhead and pray that things get better. Praying has its place. But to paraphrase Sister Mary, in Christopher Durang's play *Sister Mary Ignatius Explains It All For You*, "God answers all our prayers. Sometimes the answer is 'No!'"

After World War II, Steve's father had a hugely successful business selling sewing machines. By the late 1950s, he had stores throughout the Connecticut River Valley, from New Haven, Connecticut, to Springfield, Massachusetts. But American tastes were changing; the American economy started booming and people stopped sewing their own clothes.

By the mid-1960s, he was down to one store in Hartford and up to his neck in debt. He took a hard look at his business and realized he had four things going for him:

- His company's credit and reputation were still good.

- He had an understanding of consumer tastes.

- He knew how to sell retail and had a staff of good salespeople.

- He had ample floor space.

While he wasn't ready to make an overnight transition, he started putting a few pieces of furniture on his sewing-machine showroom floor. As he advertised the furniture (to the same demographic he'd been selling sewing machines to, blue-collar families), he gradually reduced the space for the sewing machines and increased the furniture lines. Of course, old habits (and old loves) die hard, so 20 years later, when he finally retired from his successful furniture business, there was still one sewing machine for sale in the dusty rear of his furniture store.

So if business is lousy, you start figuring out a new game plan. If life gives you lemons, make lemonade.

"Could Be Better." That's likely the answer everyone could give. And whose fault is that? If your business could be better, the only person who can make it better is you. And to do that, you need to make a plan. Which is what this entire book is about.

"Same Old, Same Old." Uh-oh. Sounds like what the dinosaurs used to say to each other just before the meteor struck (or the Great Flood, depending on your evolutionist beliefs). Department stores were doing "same old, same old" just before big-box discounters showed up. Big-box discounters were doing "same old, same old" just before the Internet showed up. Airlines like Delta and American were doing "same old, same old" just before Southwest and JetBlue showed up. Railway Express was doing "same old, same old" just before FedEx showed up.

"Same old, same old" leads to rearview-mirror vision. You start thinking that things will be okay in the future because they've been okay in the past. When banks and brokerage firms want to advertise how well they're doing, the Securities and Exchange Commission requires that they put some fine print in the ad or voiceover on the commercial: "Past performance is no guarantee of future results." Everyone who's in business should have those words posted over his or her desk. What worked today may not work tomorrow. In fact, it's a pretty good bet that what worked today won't work tomorrow.

"Great! Couldn't Be Better!" Really? Couldn't be better? Well then, be afraid—be very afraid. There was a time, around the 1930s, when the unquestioned number-one soft drink brand in the United States was Moxie. It was ubiquitous. The Moxie sign was on every neighborhood grocery store. It was sold both in bottles and in bulk as a soda fountain syrup. In fact, the name Moxie entered the English language as a noun, meaning "energy, courage, and determination." So the company decided they were so well known that there was no reason to continue advertising. Big mistake! Today, Moxie is a minor regional brand while Coca-Cola and Pepsi rule the soft drink world.

One of the truths of business is that, the more successful you are, the more tempting a target you become. Whether it's knockoffs and counterfeits; someone's figuring out how to do what you do faster, cheaper, and better; or it's changing tastes and styles, you'd better have a second act prepared and ready to go. Procter & Gamble has mastered a friendly amendment to "Great! Couldn't be better!" They're always pushing their marketing teams to improve their brands and develop new products—even though they're already number one or number two in all their categories. P&G is all about "Great. Could be better."

·   ·   ·

OKAY, SO WE lied. There's a fifth answer to the question, "How's business?" And every business should strive to give this answer: "It's great. Could be better." Nothing remains the same, so no matter what shape your business is in, you should be actively engaged in an effort to improve it. And not just by increasing your share of the market, but by remaining (or becoming) an innovative leader.

Once you adopt this positive, aspirational mindset, the first question is: What do you have to do to even start the process? And chances are, the answer is that you have to take a close look at the status quo in your organization.

Big Business, Small Business, All Business

When we looked at the successes (and failures) of new business/new product development, one of the first things we noticed was that the size of the business has no bearing on whether the 7-step process works. Each business has unique problems to surmount and unique opportunities to address, and businesses of all sizes can benefit from our process.

For big businesses, the greatest obstacles are internal inertia and internal systems. Interdisciplinary "silo busting" is tough and fraught with peril. On the other hand, big businesses have more money to allocate to R&D, testing, new product development, and rollout.

For small businesses, the biggest obstacles are R&D, testing, new product development, and rollout—and lack of resources or personnel. But on the plus side, most small businesses don't have complicated internal approval processes that can stymie new product development.

Whatever size business or style of organization you are, read all the sections of this book carefully. Know that some of our content might apply to you in depth while other advice may already be in place and part of your ongoing process. Either way, you'll need to take all the steps to get where you want to go.

The Religion Called "That's the Way We've Always Done Things"

That's a powerful religion. It's comforting. And it's dangerous. You've got to challenge it to have any chance of getting started.

Ask yourself: "What religion do I have to debunk or what sacred cow do I have to slaughter to make a new idea happen around here?" If the answer is, "The CEO," our suggestion is that you give this a shot but get your resume up to date. If the CEO doesn't approve a new product development team, it's time to move on. And if he or she is a world-class bozo, you might get fired for even suggesting it. Either way, having your own exit strategy might be necessary.

How you tackle the problem depends on your personality. You could be a Martin Luther and nail your manifesto to the CEO's door. You could be a Rasputin and start whispering in the ear of the CEO (or his/her direct report). Machiavelli. Martin Luther King, Jr. Gandhi. Dick Cheney. There is no shortage of ways to whisper in the ear of the king or to challenge the status quo. Find the way that fits your personality and fits the corporate culture.

Become a Living, Breathing Proponent of Evolution

As you're reading this (and the next several) chapters, start making notes as to how to pitch a Big Idea up the line. Obviously, the further down on the food chain you are, the trickier that's going to be. Our executive editor would like to suggest that you buy everyone in your organization—or at least everyone you want to have sign off on the idea—a copy of this book. And now that she mentioned it, we agree with her. However, you've got to know that the very *idea* of a new idea is going to be alien and uncomfortable to your management.

Start with What You Know

You know far more about new product development than you realize. Develop a presentation that asks (and answers) some basic questions:

1. Where are we heading?

2. What factors should contribute to our success?

3. What are the known threats to our success?

4. What can we "own"?

Start to ask (and answer) these questions about where the company is now, where it's heading, and where it *could* be heading. Begin by amassing a lot of not-so-subtle hints. Leave a copy of this book on the CEO's desk. Clip the articles that talk about Google's work requirement that employees devote 20 percent of their time to something they love. Start talking about GE's and P&G's model of owning businesses that are number one or number two in their category.

In other words, become a living, breathing proponent of evolution (or enlightened revolution).

Get excited. Get jazzed. Get going!

Why Rules Are Traps

THERE WAS an old saying in advertising—we haven't heard it used on TV's "Mad Men" yet—that "the second wife never trusts the secretary." Many years ago, Steve was working at the advertising agency Backer & Spielvogel on the Sony business. Backer & Spielvogel was founded by six partners who were on the Miller business at McCann Erickson. One day, the senior account, media, and creative team just pulled out of McCann and opened their doors. Shortly thereafter, the Miller brand followed.

Steve was working at B&S for Norman Tanen, and they had a great rapport with the Sony client. But the client was unhappy with the account management team. B&S replaced the account supervisor twice, and both times the client called Norman and Steve and mentioned how unhappy he was with the account executive. Now, one of the basic rules in advertising back then—spoken or not—is that "the client only talks to the account team." The third time we dutifully reported to Carl Spielvogel that Sony was unhappy with their account executive, we were handed severance checks and ordered to leave the building by 5 PM that same day. We thought we were being good soldiers. We didn't realize the client had sent us on a suicide mission. So much for rules.

In business, rules are seldom called rules. Instead, they are generally agreed-upon practices covering things like when to arrive at work (work starts at 9 AM), how to proceed at work (work until noon or 1:00, then take an hour for lunch), and when to stop (quitting time is 5 PM, whether or not you punch a time clock). But they're also understood to be the way things are done—in meetings, in the power of hierarchy, in budget and market approvals, and in annual planning. You can call it your corporate culture, but make no mistake—they're rules. But rules don't always work. (Even in the army, where it's expected there'd be no shortage of rules, there's a recognition that the rules don't always work. As enlisted men and women like to say, "Embrace the suck"—which is their rather blunt way of saying, "Deal with it.") Adhere to the rules and you can rise in the organization. Bend or break the rules—especially early in a career—and you're likely to get bounced out of the organization. When everything's going well, the basic rules work just fine. Businesses grow modestly each year, bonuses are doled out, and management rests easy. How quaint. How boring. How dumb. Because in business, standard operating procedure works less and less well every year.

If you're working for a company that's more than ten years old, you're probably operating with a set of rules (in a corporate culture) that hasn't been adopted or adapted to the new rules of the marketplace.

Changing economic, competitive, and consumer dynamics challenge businesses all the time. "Same old, same old" is a prescription for stasis, not growth. And those who repeat history are likely to find their businesses become victims of history. New, fresh, winning ideas, processes, and products and services are the stuff of the future—any and every future.

The Rule's the Limit

Rules are the domain of conventional practice, conventional thinking, conventional wisdom. But conventional wisdom is an oxymoron. If the idea or practice is conventional, how can it reside in the domain of wisdom? Conventional thinking is by definition the generally accepted way of thinking. It's widely known and available to all. There's the rub. Conventional thinking can get you just so far—about as far as it's gotten you, in fact—and in today's digital, global marketplace there's someone (in fact, probably many someones) out there ready to take what you've done and build a better mousetrap.

. . . .
CASE IN POINT

Netscape practically invented the modern browser. Virtually everyone used Netscape to access the Internet. Conventional wisdom had it that no one could derail Netscape as the gateway to the Web. But it didn't take long for Microsoft to launch Internet Explorer and bury Netscape. But that still didn't stop Firefox and Google from wading in and taking on Microsoft. Now Microsoft has countered Google with Bing. No guts, no glory!
. . . .

The browser and search wars are just a couple of examples of the hundreds of battles going on in the marketplace for share of mind and share of audience. New invention and dynamic growth come from understanding precedent. But the new, the dynamic, the phenomenal come from breaking the rules, stepping well beyond conventional practice into the exciting unknown.

New ideas are the province of disbelievers, explorers, and malcontents. Hmm, now it's getting interesting. These folks sound way more interesting. They're the people who look at what is and think about *what could be*. They operate in the pursuit and desire of something not just different but also better. They're game changers—rule breakers passionately seeking to find something superior. For change agents, rules are uncomfortable. They feel anxious and constrained that doing the same thing over and over again just won't work. It's a dead end.

. . . .

CASE IN POINT

Apple's "Think Different" campaign celebrated inventors, artists, and political risk takers—a range of pioneers and iconoclasts who broke the rules to achieve great things in products and social change. The campaign was big, literally (as huge billboards) and figuratively (with its large presumption). It struck a pose as the personal computer for giants and would-be giants—for people with Big Ideals and Big Ideas. It found its voice in inspiring television commercials. It embraced cities and highways in huge, larger-than-life billboards.

And it broke a fundamental grammatical rule to boot. The correct adverb is "differently." But "Think different" was an admonition and an invitation—a modern update to Apple's groundbreaking 1984 commercial that introduced Macintosh to the world in one airing only—during the 1984 Super Bowl. It was also a dig at computer giant IBM, which had been using the tag line "Think" since Thomas Watson first brought it over to the company way back when it was still the Computer Tabulating Recording Company.

. . . .

The Research Requirement . . . and Trap

We're going to assume that your company has some kind of research methodology in place—some way to tap into the voice of your customer and get a feel for your products, your services, your brand, or your message.

If you're a Fortune 500 company, you probably have a well-staffed research department and a Chief Research Officer (CRO), or some such vaunted title. In a world where consumer attitudes and ever-elusive consumer touch points are moving so fast and changing so dramatically, research is critical. You want to know: Is what you're putting out there authentic? Credible? Compelling? Connecting? If it isn't—in the two-way world of digital communication—you'll hear about it. You'll get ridiculed and slammed, blogged to death by consumer critics who are ever-vigilant for and vocal about dumb or insulting ideas. And you'll get the message fast, loud, and painfully. Good research can provide great guidance based on what customers know and feel.

If you're a medium-size organization, you should be monitoring all that information through third-party research that you subscribe to or buy on a regular basis. If you're a small business or SOHO operator, it's even more critical that you keep an ear tuned to customer attitudes. Even if it's as basic as conducting a customer-satisfaction survey each year or using Survey-Monkey or another on-line tool.

The dilemma is that Big Ideas—really Big Ideas—often defy the ability to get a clear or clean read from customers who don't have a reference point for the innovation. How can you measure what doesn't exist yet? This is the trap and the danger of research—it can't easily answer the question of what might be.

. . . .

CASE IN POINT

Imagine if Arm & Hammer Baking Soda researched the idea that you could/should stick an entire box of their baking ingredient into your fridge to eliminate odors. From a research standpoint, consumers would likely flatly reject the idea. The odor-liberating product benefit was way outside the expectation of the brand's credentials. And yet, the Arm & Hammer Baking Soda revelation and product extension increased brand usage geometrically.

Arm & Hammer Baking Soda is the poster child for Big Idea thinking. Putting a box in the refrigerator and another in the freezer as deodorizers had nothing whatsoever to do with its name or original purpose. Everyone had a box of Arm & Hammer Baking Soda in his/her kitchen cabinet. And they used it three times a year—a couple of teaspoons at a time—to bake a cake. But this new, secondary usage became its primary reason for being. And a box-at-a-time every few months became a business game changer, moving usage explosively beyond a couple of teaspoons twice a year.

. . . .

No Roadmaps or GPS

The Arm & Hammer story has a happy ending. So does the not-so-sticky 3M Post-it story (which we'll discuss later). New ideas don't have a roadmap. They're big and new because they haven't been done before. With a new idea, we've never seen or heard of the kind of product or service use that's being offered. We don't intuitively understand its usage or how consumer uptake will happen. We don't know what a Big Idea looks like, tastes like, sounds like, smells like, or feels like. How do we come to our senses about a Big Idea? Because if it's a genuinely Big Idea with a great piece of communication behind it, it will make plenty of sense when it comes to market! But would you know it if you saw it?

· ·

CASE IN POINT

Light beer seemed like a pretty lame idea when it first came to market. Gablinger's was the first light beer, and it was a colossal failure. Why? Not because light beer was a bad idea, but because the benefit proposition for light beer wasn't made clear—and worse, the brew tasted terrible. The ante for new product break-throughs in existing categories is that they must meet the basic benefit criterion of the category. Beer has got to taste good.

Miller Lite became the breakthrough entry in a new light beer category because, from a marketing and advertising standpoint, they figured out what to do right: First, the beer tasted good—the minimum cost of entry. Second, their benefit proposition beyond good taste—"Less filling"—was neither a diet nor a calorie claim. It was a drinking claim. You could drink more. You could have more fun. You could get more drunk. The Miller Lite sports celebrity campaign pitted parallel opponents against one another arguing the two key benefits of Miller Lite, "Less filling. Tastes great." It broke the rules of beer advertising. And, it built a business and new category.

· ·

"Less filling?" What an odd claim for a diet beer. No self-respecting guy wants to drink diet beer. But the marketing and name gave them product permission to drink more. Now you're on to something. But the claim—which seemed so logical—defied conventional wisdom. No guts, no glory. To reap really big rewards, you've got to break the rules, shift the paradigms, find new ways to talk about innovative ideas—and connect with your consumers. You get the idea.

The New Rules

A FEW YEARS ago, one of Steve's co-workers came to him for advice. Steve used to race cars, and this co-worker was planning to do it himself and wanted some practical tips. Steve asked him if he knew the test as to whether or not a person could race cars. When this associate said no, Steve took him to the men's room.

"How much money do you have in your wallet?" Steve asked.

"About forty dollars."

"Take out a twenty-dollar bill" (which he did). "Now flush it down the toilet."

"I can't do that."

"Then you can't race cars."

About a year later, this associate came to Steve and said, "Of all the advice I got, yours was the only correct information."

Could you flush a $20 bill down the toilet right now? If not, you may not be able to be part of a new product development team.

Break any rules lately? It's never too late to start. Because if you're planning to come up with some breakthrough ideas, you've got to be willing to break the rules.

Breaking the rules is tricky. And the older we get, the more averse we likely become to tampering with the status quo. Rule breaking is risky. You can get caught and punished or maybe even worse—embarrassed. But breaking the rules can also be incredibly liberating. As teenagers, most of us tried it. Running a stop sign. Graffiti on a wall. Toilet paper on a house. Halloween stunts. Doughnuts in a field. Maybe you even ramped it up to the level of criminal mischief. But beyond the momentary thrill, what's that all about? Yes, you can always break rules to challenge authority, but if that's your only reason it's just going to land you in jail, get you fired—or create a product or service that nobody wants.

Breaking the rules for a positive purpose is hard work. It requires discipline and, ironically, establishing a new set of rules. New paradigms and platforms create new ways of considering products and services and new ways of connecting with consumers. There are a number of disciplines you can follow to get from A to B, or should we say from A to 3 or A to Peach? The new path will jump the curb of logic to follow a different route to dynamic thinking and dramatic business growth.

The Gen Y Dilemma

One of the main reasons to consider breaking the rules is the new generation of consumers. We're facing an interesting disconnect in business between the new 20-something workforce and their supervisors. As echo boomers, today's 20-somethings are self-absorbed, self-centered, and self-satisfied.

Generation Y doesn't want to follow the rules. They didn't create them or grow up with them. They don't understand the logic of a lot of the behaviors they're being asked to copy or emulate. They observe that many of today's—err yesterday's—business practices don't make a whole lot of sense. Are they spoiled and selfish? Maybe. But, do they have a point about challenging the authority of means and methods that just don't make sense to them? Likely so.

The everyday conventions of business lifestyle just don't reflect the dynamic changes we're seeing today in consumers and marketplaces. Increasingly, consumers are "checking out" of the same old sales pitches and product and service selections. Consumer loyalty is at an all-time low. Digital media provide consumers with an everyday bullshit test and a two-way mechanism for customers to tell businesses exactly what they think. The powerful mommy blog network is rebelling at being manipulated to shill for products and services.

That's why you're probably seeing a flattening in your business sales—and why you keep reading more and more success stories that involve the Internet, social media, and ways of marketing that you never dreamed of just 10 years ago.

· ·

CASE IN POINT

The people at McNeil-PPC thought they were on to a good idea for Motrin when they put a commercial on the Web touting the efficacy of Motrin in alleviating back pain for moms who carry their babies around. Within hours of posting the new commercial, the mommy blog network was all over it. Blog after blog talked about how offensive the message was. How dare Motrin tell moms about what to do and not to do when it came to caring for and bonding with their babies? Who were these corporate shills to encroach upon caregiving?

Within four days, Motrin pulled the commercial and the entire home page of their site was dedicated to a profound apology for its offense. Who would have thought? Motrin simply thought they were on to a good idea regarding extended usage of the painkiller. Wow, did they learn a lesson about vetting ideas with consumers. What followed was a warm, fuzzy, and personal message on the Motrin Web site: "Hi, We've learned a lot from our consumers lately and continue to listen. We are working on a path forward, more to come on this. Stay tuned . . . . Best, Jenna and Stephanie, Product Directors of Motrin and Children's Motrin." Lesson learned—and business practice changed, likely forever. Consumer feedback is now an essential component of the brand proposition.

• •

Consumers are changing. The way they operate in the world is changing. They're much more active and activist. And they have the communication vehicles to state their case. So you've got to embrace their new ways of thinking and new ways of creating their own rules if you want to win their hearts, minds, and wallets. And it's not just big packaged-goods customers. We're willing to bet no matter how small or specialized your business is, your customers are changing as well. For openers, do you notice how different clients like to be communicated with in different ways? Some clients will return your phone calls—and ignore your e-mails. Others will respond to texting but never check their voice mail. One of the most basic things you've got to do for your business is to determine the way your different customers want to be spoken to and then talk to them in their language and on their platform(s) of choice.

As you start to think about what kind of breakthrough idea you're going to look for, consider these different ways of catching the attention of your audience.

Border Crossing

One method for breaking the rules is what we call "border crossing." Presumably, you know the brand geography you own. But, what's over the fence or across the border that's appealing and accessible? Can you extend your brand portfolio to logical places that provide added customer service or enhance consumer experience?

. . . .
CASE IN POINT

UPS was in the shipping business. We would see their trucks everywhere and we would receive packages from them. But without brick-and-mortar locations, how many consumers had any idea how to use UPS to ship a package? The acquisition of Mail Boxes, Etc. solved the dilemma. Rebranded as UPS Stores, these locations put another face on UPS and provided a place to go—competitive with the post office—with ready access and fulfillment of the company promise "What can brown do for you?" Changing the playing field also forced their competitors to respond. FedEx was forced to pay a premium for the Kinko's stores—even though the corporate culture of Kinko's was

nowhere near that of FedEx—which they then took years to
rebrand as FedEx Office.

• •

Benchmarketing

Benchmarking is the art of studying other businesses. What do other businesses do well that we admire—in our category or in other business disciplines? Are there aspects of the other guy's brand proposition or customer connection that we can adopt and adapt to our business? The coffee wars have seen the fast-food chains take a chapter out of the Starbucks playbook by offering premium-blend coffee. Benchmarking leads to new marketing—which we call "benchmarketing."

• •

CASE IN POINT

Coffee was never a driver of the McDonald's business proposition. But coffee is a high-margin product that has experienced a renaissance, thanks to Starbucks and Dunkin' Donuts. Benchmarketing has put teeth into the McDonald's coffee business. They upgraded their coffee to a premium blend and have been using a new coffee story to attract more morning business. The other fast-food chains are following, and as we write this there's an all-out coffee war going on for share of market—or should we say share of sip?

• •

Lower Cost of Entry

Another winning rule breaker is lower cost of entry: on a permanent basis or as a promotion—cents off, bonus packs, loading promotions. You don't have to be first into a growing category to play. A satisfying option that offers a competitive price to encourage trial, blunt your competition, or just build competitive noise can bring some attractive share gains.

Our coffee example is also true for lower cost of entry. The fast-food guys were already serving coffee. The cost to McDonald's of upgrading their brew offering was nominal. A bean is a bean. They're competing on the coffee platform and trying to beat the specialists—Starbucks and Dunkin' Donuts—on price. Coffee margins are attractive. Starbucks coffee is expensive. Offer a lower priced beverage in a branded environment that extends brand permission for java expertise and voilà, Starbucks and Dunkin' Donuts have a major new competitor vying for that critical morning business. A cup of joe for a buck—every day at McDonald's. Hmm.

Now consider the dynamism of combining benchmarketing with border crossing. You can preempt a business or brand by learning what they do well and emulating it on your own terms and your own turf.

. . . .

CASE IN POINT

McDonald's has had its McCafé subbrand since 1993. It started in Australia and spread to several other countries. But in the United States, McDonald's did very little with the brand until recently. They have now put teeth into McCafé with an expanded, branded coffee menu. The McCafé "border crossing" has real costs attached to it and requires significant capital investment, but it lives in McDonald's stores, extends the brand reputation, and invites an influx of new customers into the stores. Breakfast at McDonald's gets an added incentive. And imagine the uptake on the Egg McMuffin!

. . . .

Radar Sneaking

The sneaky launch is one of the most gratifying rule breakers out there. The burden here is that you've got to be good. Steve Jobs is the poster child for under-the-radar innovation. Sneaking in under the radar can be accomplished in many ways: manifested as a new business, in advertising, or as partnerships. Jobs has played all of these cards.

• •

CASE IN POINT

Back in 1984, the launch of the Macintosh computer was a Super Bowl event. A $1 million commercial entitled "1984" ran one time only, during the TV broadcast of the 1984 Super Bowl. It was the talk of the game (who even remembers who played?) and has continued to be talked about, watched online, and studied for north of 25 years as a brilliant hijack of traditional PCs. It was a market maker that set the table for Macintosh expertise in laptop innovation.

• •

To this day, Apple remains the master of under-the-radar buzz on the Internet. All of their "sneak attacks" are carefully coordinated with judicious leaks to the bloggers who follow Apple on the Web—building buzz and interest strategically before the new products are introduced. The rumors that circulate are usually right. And the timing preempts competition and builds news and noise that eclipse the cost of advertising.

Fast forward a few years. Jobs stepped away from Apple and started dabbling in the computer animation business, setting a new standard for animated movie features with Pixar Animation Studios. *Toy Story*, *Finding Nemo*, *The Incredibles*, *Up*, and numerous other Pixar masterpieces combined great story lines with brilliant computer imagery. The company's offerings were so successful that the master of animation, the Walt Disney Company, moved from distributing Pixar movies to acquiring the business. Pixar changed the animation business and energized feature-length animation into becoming a major source of family entertainment and movie industry profit—and a new Academy Award category!

. . . .

CASE IN POINT

The world wasn't waiting for yet another MP3 player, but Apple's benchmarketing in the music business was not just about a better MP3 player. In fact, many critics contend that the iPod is an inferior machine to any number of other competitors. But their now symbolic white earbuds zagged against the zig of black electronics. And the genius of iPod wasn't just the elegant design. It was the radar-sneaking back room called iTunes. This was not just another MP3 player. Jobs created an integrated online music experience and store. No longer just in the computer business, Apple Computer changed its name to Apple Inc.

Then there is the incredible success story of the iPhone. Rumor had it that Apple was going to get into the mobile phone business. In the early days, there were as many detractors as there were believers. Why would Apple venture into a crowded market where new bells and whistles were being innovated all the time, offered up by players with mobile phone credentials? Who did Apple think they were to take on Nokia, Motorola, LG, Samsung, and the other mobile giants? The world had plenty of capable phones from reputable companies in the cellular space.

But Apple wasn't about to bring a me-too phone to market. The iPhone extended an all-new user interface that appealed to the passions of Apple fans, but also to an entirely new fan base of people who would carry their iPhones as badges of early adopter cool. Many, in the early days of the phone, did not even have iPhone connectivity or integration with their office e-mail, but the cool power of iPhone made it a must-have accessory— and iPhone applications (apps) have become a game-changer in the mobile phone business. Google, which seemed to have the Midas touch with new services and software, has struggled to launch its Android phone operating system because the first question consumers now ask in phone stores is, "How many apps are available?"

Greetings, Pardner!

Very often the new rules of breaking the rules can take a brand or company into territory they don't—or even can't—own. That's the time and turf for working with partners. Strategic alliances can be a win-win for the paradigm buster.

To get to market in the mobile business, Apple needed a partner. Sure, they could build a great device. But they weren't in the telephone service business. The AT&T deal set the table for Apple and burnished languishing credentials for AT&T in mobile (where other cellular players had better reputations and superior coverage). A five-year exclusive tie-up was a long-term deal, but it gave Apple the access they needed to the market and the power to program their iPhones for a new type of service (apps), and it gave AT&T the security and competitive insulation to rebuild a user base among people who just had to have an iPhone.

To the Victor Belongs the Spoils

Pixar is still making state-of-the-art animation. Its inclusion in the Walt Disney Company has restored Disney to the pinnacle of animation. Apple computers are growing in share of market, and Apple is still viewed as the innovator in the laptop business. The iPod continues to be innovative in styles and iTunes has set the pricing standards for song downloads. The iTouch offers iPhone credentials, capabilities, and navigation without the phone. The iPhone is in its third generation; Apple's App store insulates the iPhone from new touch-screen competitors (e.g., Blackberry Storm and Palm Pre), just as iTunes did for iPod.

Apple Inc.'s magic in rule breaking continually resets expectations of what a company can accomplish when they set their sights beyond conventional wisdom. Offer what everyone expects and the business opportunity will be just that: expected—and likely, small and unimpressive. Extend consumer experience through inspired rule breaking and look for exciting innovation in new products and services that will yield rewards greater than ever imagined.

• • •

SO, LET'S summarize: As you start to build your plan for establishing a rule-breaking team/process in your company, you'll want to explore a number of possible avenues. Each one of them represents both risks and rewards—and each has to be explored in depth to uncover the mother lode:

- Border crossing
- Radar sneaking

- Benchmarketing

- Lower cost of entry

- Partnering

Keep these all in mind and refer back to this chapter when you get to the section on developing your Big Idea.

STEP TWO

Get Business Buy-In

4

Build the Sale

PAUL HAD A client at Procter & Gamble (P&G) who rewarded
risk taking. He believed risk taking could be activated at all
levels of the organization, at any level of a person's career. He
was as disciplined and dedicated to the operating principles of
P&G success as anyone else in the organization. But he
rewarded the risk takers each year with what he called the
Turtle Award. The plaque depicted a turtle on top of a roaring
fire, with its head sticking out. It was humorous and treacherous.
Stick your head out and get incinerated in the inferno or set fire
to a brilliant idea. He encouraged his youngest charges with the
opportunity for winning the award. And he made it very clear

that the system was big enough, the checks and balances strong enough that the flaming turtles would either quietly burn out or could become the stuff of P&G's greatest inventions.

If only every company had management players who sought out and rewarded the innovators. In most cases, the idea of pursuing new ideas is given lip service, but when it comes to evaluations, managers are measured by how well they stay the course and implement the plan. Innovators need to be very careful and savvy when navigating the waters of change. Without management buy-in, the prospect of innovating—let alone implementing—an exciting change will likely be dead on arrival.

As you read the next two chapters, make margin notes. We're going to ask you a bunch of questions—and you should jot down the immediate, instinctive answers that pop into your mind.

■　■　■

SO WHAT'S AN innovator to do? At any level of the organization, you've got to build the sale! What does that mean? It means that you've got to put together a selling proposition and a selling presentation to get management buy-in.

It's a creative act. How can you present the idea of doing new things in new ways to get new results without management's thinking you're taking your eye off the ball? For openers, you've got to do your job at least as well—if not better—than anyone else.

Don't put your day job at risk. Do your job as prescribed. In fact, to have any shot at making this happen, you'll have to do your regular job even better than expected. No one's going to take you seriously about a Big Idea search if you're not even managing your day-in, day-out workload. Critical to building the sale of something new is to provide management the confidence that everything is in hand. You're on plan, managing expectations and achieving the goals outlined in your plan. You're doing your day job. But you've got an idea that can take your business, or some portion of the business, well beyond the set plan and goals.

Some of the support for your presentation might come from your own sales force. Get some anecdotal (or numerical) evidence from the people in the field. What feedback are they getting? Is sales resistance growing? If so, why? Is competition outflanking you? Are there some early-warning signs that your current business model might not be sustainable? Are some of your products losing their luster? We're not talking about a Chicken Little presentation ("The sky is falling! The sky is falling!"), but we are suggesting that any smart insight backed up by good evidence will help make the sale.

Do a Web search. Find articles that support your case. Summarize them and footnote them in the appendix of your presentation.

Outline . . . Always Outline

Start with a simple question: what are you looking to do? Is this just a question of refreshing the brand? Developing a new service? Creating a new way of doing business with suppliers? We understand that you don't have the Big Idea yet, but you still need to build some framework to support your intentions. What ballpark do you want to play in to come up with the idea? Express it in the most appealing and accessible way possible—it'll help you make the sale. If there's no clear understanding of what you're trying to accomplish, you have no chance of getting a green light to proceed.

· ·
CASE IN POINT

A number of years ago, when Tom Peters's and Bob Water-man's book In Search of Excellence *was produced as a PBS television special, the program followed the team at 3M that was proposing the company go into the CD manufacturing business. The team was aware that the medium was totally alien to 3M's understanding of what the company did. When the team made its presentation to the board, it held up a sample CD–and made a point of holding it on its edge. What the board saw was a thin surface rather than a round disc that looked like an old 45 rpm record. The development team recognized that management was familiar with "thin" items like tape–audio tape, adhesive tape, etc.–so by holding the disc on its edge, the team made the disc "familiar" to management. It wanted management to think, "Oh, it's thin, like our other products. We know how to make thin things." A subtle move that helped make the sale.*

· ·

What do you need to accomplish your plan? What do you want from management? What will the approval be? As you look to become a change agent, you need to figure out what will put you on the best path. If you're operating within any kind of organization, you're going to need support where it matters—from the higher ups. And that means management, the people who can say yes and have the means—did someone say budget, team, and time?—to support your adventure. Know who they are and how you're going to make your case. Pre-sell them. Get them sympathetic and favorable to your intentions in advance.

An outline is the critical first step to building any selling presentation. There are several questions you need to ask yourself in putting together your outline.

1. Who are you going to be selling/presenting to?

   – How many levels of management are involved?

   – Will you have to sell your immediate supervisor first? (Duh—chances are he or she isn't going to let you blithely set a meeting with the CEO.)

   – Are there side presentations and allies you need to enlist? (Like the head of research and the chief financial officer. Good call, there; those two could be your biggest allies or enemies.)

2. What are you selling? What's your Big Idea? (Note, we're not saying you've already come up with the Big Idea—your Big Idea at this point is the idea of assembling a team to come up with the Big Idea—get it?)

   – What's your rationale for why chasing the development of the idea is such a powerful opportunity and possible business winner?

   – Who will you need? Who do you think will make up your team?

3. What response are you looking for?

   – What does a yes look like?

   – What do you need to activate your idea?

4. What's your promise to management?

- How are you going to measure and report your progress?

- What are their approval points? Cut-off points? Be sure to let them know they'll still have control.

These are some key considerations in drafting your outline and building your presentation. Your outline is highly personal and variable. It's driven by and needs to be responsive to your business culture. It needs to clear, complete, and compelling. This is a tough sell so you need to build the best presentation ever. You need your audience to love the opportunity you're presenting—from the very first page, slide, or opening words. Incite enthusiasm! Start a fire! Build heat. Then, build from there.

Who Are You Selling?

One of the first questions you need to ask yourself is who the best point of entry is for your eventual idea. Is it your immediate boss? A mentor? A corporate strategist? Someone in another department? The CEO's wife or kid? The answer should be twofold:

1. Who is most likely to be a really important supporter?

2. Who is likely to be your optimal "idea ambassador," who can help advance your idea without getting you in trouble because you broke protocol?

These may be the same people or they may be a couple of allies who can help you navigate the tricky currents to reach new shores. Figuring out the sales path within the organization is key. One no and your idea could be killed. Important small yeses along the way will build traction and momentum, and will likely cause positive buzz within the organization.

What Are You Selling?

More often than not, you'll want to focus on a method for change rather than a single idea. Single ideas will win or lose on the merits of the rationale. You can advance that stuff anytime—and should as a matter of course. It's simply good business practice. But what we're talking about here is more fundamental change: the pursuit of Big Ideas (plural) through new means and methods for discovery, evaluation, and implementation. We're talking about game-changing ideas. We're talking about the on-the-face-of-it "That'll never sell" stuff, the stuff of disbelievers that comes—after the fact—to make believers of us all!

What Are You Looking For?

You need to be very clear not only about the idea you're selling but also the deliverable you want from your sales pitch. Are you looking to spearhead a new business process? Do you want to lead a think tank? Are you looking to be part of an interdisciplinary team to streamline new ideas? Are you looking for time off from your current responsibilities? Are you seeking a specific team? Do you need a budget? How much? What kind of plan are you planning to operate against? What are the key benchmarks against which your enterprise should be measured? What amount of time and what key metrics do you want to provide confidence along the way that show your initiative is on track?

What Do You Need?

When you put your outline and subsequent selling presentation together, what are you going to ask for? What do you need? From whom do you need it? What permission do you want to succeed *or* to fail? Don't embark on any change-agent escapade without the confidence that there is enough rope to pull yourself safely back to shore, not one that's so short you might just hang yourself with it. Even failure needs to be planned and viewed as a noble attempt at something great, not a harebrained waste of time that gets you fired.

How Long Will It Take?

Scott Adams's Dilbert cartoon strip is filled with humorous takes on the idea that management wants to measure the time required to come up with a completely unknown idea. But you've got to give them some kind of time frame.

Don't be in a rush to be a hero. As the saying goes, "Under-promise and overdeliver." It's a lot smarter to tell them it will take ten months and do it in seven than to tell them six months and have to beg for an extra 30 days. (By the way, even the way you specify your time frame can make a huge difference. It's human nature to think of 12 months as being much shorter than one year, just as it might be smarter to say, "one hundred twenty days" rather than "four months.")

In the early days of Amazon.com, Paul placed his first order for some books, unsure of what the consumer experience would be. Immediately, he was notified that his books would likely arrive within seven days. That felt pretty good; seven days is not a long time. And the "within" made the promise feel even shorter. When the books arrived in three days, Paul was impressed. It was part of what made him a repeat customer. Amazon.com is very good at the customer equation of under-promising and overdelivering. Customers reward them for that with repeat orders.

Who Will You Need on Your Team?

Who do you want to help enable the vision? And how much of their time do you require? Again, that's going to depend on what you're shooting for. If you're hoping to come out with a low-carbon-footprint, extra jumbo-size version of your product, you're going to need your packaging engineers. If you're planning to create a competitor to the iPhone, you're going to need a whole lotta designers and programmers. If you're looking to develop a delicious low-fat, low-calorie snack food, you're going to need food scientists and nutritionists. This is why we say you should try to involve as many divisions of the company as possible when you first propose the idea. You'll be surprised (pleasantly) at the number of people in other departments and divisions who will want to help bring big new ideas to life. People like a challenge and an opportunity. And they especially like to step away from their everyday tasks to take on a new opportunity or solve a problem.

How Much Money Will You Need?

What's the budget you require to bring your plan to life? Don't lowball it lest you have to come back for more money sooner than you think! Again, underpromise and overdeliver. It's a lot smarter to ask for more than you need so you don't have to keep going back to the well. (And what you think of as more than you need will virtually never be the case; you'll need every cent of the budget you get.) Besides, there's nothing like an annoyed CFO to kill a viable idea simply because you needed an unanticipated $10,000.

Be sure to include any bonuses and incentives you will want to offer members of your team. You also should include the cost of rewards for anyone in the company who submits ideas for your consideration, as well as larger rewards for ideas that are accepted.

What's Your Promise?

What are the key goals and milestones? And how are you going to measure your success against them? Nobody's going to write you a blank check. You want to be sure that you become the toughest critic of your process and progress rather than having impatient management breathing down your neck.

That said, no risk, no reward! If you're going to play the Big Idea quest game, you need to be just as imaginative in your disciplined approach as you are wild and free in your quest. Define the process. And provide a clear roadmap of the steps toward innovation. That's your promise—that you will be expeditious in your venture, inclusive in your adventure, and responsible in reaching your milestones and checking your metrics along the way. There's always risk that in failure you'll falter, but if you play it all well, your value to the company will be enhanced—even in failure—if your process, commitment, and communication are clear and compelling.

5

Make It Stick

WHEN PAUL'S father Shep was a kid, every Saturday was nego-
tiate-a-movie day. Shep wanted nothing more than to go to the
matinee to see the latest movie—including the previews and the
Flash Gordon serial installment. It was never a given that he would
be able to go. It was a project, a sales pitch. He knew exactly what
he needed to do to get a yes from his mom. The case needed to be
made early and often. The growing nag needed to be sufficiently
well tuned that it advanced his objective without triggering his
mom's wrath. He enjoyed an excellent track record of completing
his sale and getting to the movies, week after week. Kids are
innately good at this. Observe how they make a sale!

So you've figured out what you want to sell. You have a clear sense of where support lies within the organization and who is going to be on your side to help advance your plan. Now it's time to make the sale and make it stick.

Your selling presentation is ready to go. You want to practice it in front of people you trust, who don't have a yes or no vote. Is it as clear as it can be? Is it short and simple? Compelling and complete?

Is your selling presentation engaging and inclusive? Have you built in memorable nuggets of insight? Is there an implicit—if not explicit—elevator speech in the sales pitch? Is it the kind of presentation that will generate buzz? Will your boss go home at night, excited about it, and tell his or her spouse? You want all of this and more.

Rehearse. And then rehearse again. And again. Out loud. In front of an audience of allies. Get their comments and constructive feedback. This presentation could be the performance of your career!

Champions

Every idea needs believers and champions. Have you built the presentation in such a way that those from whom you seek a yes are empowered to feel that they're partners in the idea's creation? Does it suggest that anyone who shares your vision can be swept up in the rewards of hoped-for success? As you go up the line seeking approvals, the key is to build believers and allies along the way. These people become partners in your idea. No need to be a gunslinging, hot-shot, one-person show. The ego game is counterproductive. Be a team player. You want fans and stakeholders.

Sharing the vision and the ownership of the idea gives you a much-increased opportunity to get affirmation along the way to the ultimate approval. You need to advance your idea slowly, carefully, and consistently throughout the organization. After all, this is not just another approval. This is about changing the rules of the game for how your company operates and how you will operate within it.

CEO or No Go

Given that you're looking to make a major change in the way your company does business (Oh, did we not mention that?), you're going to need to get your presentation all the way to the top—even if you don't personally get the chance to take it there. It's CEO or no go. By that we mean even if the Chief Marketing Officer signs off on the initiative, his "business life expectancy" is only about 16 months. It would be a colossal shame if your idea dies with his short tenure after you put a huge amount of sweat and toil into a great idea. You need champions. And you need them deep and high throughout the organization.

In fact, you want nothing less than exuberant interest in what you are doing from the most junior people in the organization to the C-suite players who should be cheering you on to succeed big time.

Game Day for the Selling Presentation

It's one thing to write a great presentation. It's something far different to set the stage for the presentation's receiving its best audience. Think carefully about who you want in the room each time you present. Decide where the presentation should be made. Is it someone's office? A conference room? Offsite some-where? What props have you built into the presentation and why? Keep in mind that if the presentation feels like every other business pitch, you'll find it tougher to achieve belief in your innovation. "Same old, same old" will leave people believing that you are going to produce "same old, same old" as well. To make people feel you are doing something different, present differently! (Or, in Apple-speak, "Present Different!")

In his *Little Blue Book of Advertising*, Steve's partner Jeff Woll tells a story about the most successful new business pitch he was ever involved with. The agency was going after a brokerage firm—an industry that, at the time, was notorious for boring, cookie-cutter advertising. The agency team assembled every ad they could find from every competitor, as well as from the brokerage firm itself. They papered the walls of their conference room with these ads—but cut out the logos so no one could identify which company did which ad. When the marketing team from the brokerage firm showed up for the presentation, they were asked to match the ads on the wall to the different competitors. And some of the team couldn't even identify their own ads!

It's an ad ploy that's been used many times. But in that meeting, it was new to the client and painted a painfully compelling picture of the sameness of category advertising. Our point? A little theatricality can't hurt. Everyone wants to be romanced, and there's nothing like a little drama—relevant selling drama!

The Ask

Don't ever let a good presentation go to waste. Make sure it ends with a clear resolution. What do you want? At each level of the presentation, what you're asking for may be different. In the early meetings, the ask may be as simple as support for scheduling the next level meeting. But in *every* meeting, the ultimate ask must be articulated as well. What commitment are you looking for? It's about time, team, and money. Think hard about the ask for each and every meeting. To falter could mean to lose momentum or, worse, the sale.

The Idea

As we said in the last chapter, we know you don't have the Big Idea yet, but you've got to give your audience something to think about—some context in which your enterprise will operate, some vision of what you might create. Will you be looking to go green? Reduce production costs? Identify line extensions? Create a whole new product? Streamline R&D? Identify strategic partners or acquisition candidates? Develop a new industry? Shift the focus of the company's business? Your vision can be as big as you think the audience can accept (and as big as you believe you can meaningfully and successfully take on)—but you've got to give them something to go on.

Steve had a boss—Bob Sherman—who was a master salesman. In fact, he was far less interested in the idea than he was in the thrill of the sale. What Bob would do is bring two or three people (max) to the client presentation. He would present to the lowest-level person who had to approve the ad. Once he made the sale—usually fairly easily because the person at that level was way overmatched—he would suggest that they all go to that person's boss's office. Immediately. When they arrived at the boss's office, he now had the subordinate as an ally, not a presentee. So the underling became part of the sales team, helping Bob make the sale. He would continue this process—sometimes over the course of two or three days and numerous meetings—until they arrived at the senior-most person's office. By that time, Bob might have seven or eight people in tow. But all of them were already sold and would help him make the sale to the senior person. Smart.

Same story, different dynamic. Paul always wanted to be sure a client attended agency commercial shoots. These clients became major ambassadors for the sale. After all, they were at the production, they knew everything that was shot, they had a unique appreciation of the rough cut, and they were a powerful selling voice with the higher ups in their organizations.

Making a Sale That Sticks

What does commitment look like? Feel like? Surely you need to engage and feel real excitement about your plan. There needs to be deep belief in your new vision—a "wow" factor of support that will enable your great new idea to emerge.

It's critical that you anticipate the level of acceptance your idea can garner. Don't delude yourself into thinking that lukewarm acceptance is carte blanche. Often what is *unsaid* in support is even more critical than what is said. Without deep, enthusiastic buy-in your plan will get torpedoed faster than you can imagine. The first setback will be the excuse to cancel the project.

There's nothing worse than a good idea put on a track that's too short. Pressing on the brakes before you're able to get moving is a common problem in business. It's a tragic dilemma in planning for innovation in organizational cultures that want immediate, tangible results. The sale must be made deep and the commitment to the process and support must take priority over ongoing "you can't do that" doubts that confront the process at every turn. So swing for the fences both in your proposal and in your ask. But accompany all of that with huge enthusiasm for what you believe the endgame opportunity can be. The goal is nothing short of wild excitement for what you are doing. Get real commitment, build a groundswell for that buy-in, or just retreat and go back to doing things the way you always have. Alas.

. . . .

CASE IN POINT

The phenomenon of 3M's Post-it Notes didn't just happen. Yeah, it was the famous error in the lab that created an adhesive that didn't have the sticking power to be permanent. It was the inventor (Spencer Silver) and in-company promoter (Arthur Fry) who intuited a use for a paper that could stick and restick without damaging the surface it stuck to, but they had to figure out a way to sell the behavioral need and customer opportunity to management.

The groundswell that enabled the invention to find its way to the world was the distribution of pads of Post-it Notes to lower level people in the organization who got swept up with their utility and who made them a pervasive presence in the office. Everyone who used the notes became a vital ambassador of the invention. The rest is history.

. . . .

Start to build your case. Know that you may not make the sale in the current fiscal year—but don't let that discourage you. Take all the examples we give in this book, and any others you can think of, and start to build the case, brick by brick, until you've got a proposition management just can't ignore.

STEP THREE

Organize the Team
and Process

True Believers, Consensus Builders, and Odd Ducks

IT'S TEMPTING to make your best general the head of the combined forces—and it would be a big mistake. If George Patton had been the Supreme Allied Commander in Europe during the Second World War, we wouldn't have stopped at Berlin. If Montgomery had led the troops, we'd still be in France, trying to decide whether it's safe to cross the Rhine.

Great field officers don't make great strategic commanders. And great strategic commanders don't make great field officers, either. In business, it's known as the Peter Principle: The better someone is at a particular skill, the more likely it is that person will be promoted beyond his or her skill level.

Churchill and Roosevelt chose Dwight Eisenhower—a senior general from the supply and logistics side of the military—to be Supreme Allied Commander. Most important, he was a diplomat and consensus builder. He was someone who was able to win the trust and respect of the strong egos who would report to him.

That's the kind of team leader you want. Not a glory warrior but a company line officer. Someone who's passionate about the business and is itching to get the opportunity to unleash the full brand potential of your business. Take a quick read of the business book *Good to Great,* by Jim Collins. Read the author's analysis of the CEO type who is ideal to move a company from good to great. That "Level 5" player is the person you want to manage your new product team. A person who might be five to eight years away from becoming CEO of your company, but has the insight, passion, and commitment to the business, as well as a fire in the belly.

"I'm a one-man band."

You can do this by yourself—but you can also benefit by pulling together an advisory board of people who know you, know your business, and have a good sense of what your strengths and weaknesses are.

We have a friend who had a successful private practice as a chiropractor. But he recognized that he couldn't build a business he could retire on if he just kept it as a one-person, word-of-mouth practice. So every five years he would gather a war room of a half-dozen business associates in other fields: marketers, advertisers, and finance people, and he would do a half-day planning session on how to grow and develop his business.

We all got free chiropractic care. He got to retire at 57.

Team, Not Just Leader

If you're the leader—or if you've picked a leader—you've now got to put together the team. Assembling the team is a critical step in enabling, engaging, and empowering new ideas. It doesn't happen by asking an existing group to come up with a new idea. Existing teams have a lot at stake in maintaining the status quo. No one wants to allocate precious resources (people and budget) hunting for an idea that may never come to life and isn't part of their job responsibility. That's not what they're paid for or charged with doing. Seems weird, but they're all about staying the course and implementing the plan.

So recognize that you're going to have to put the team together from different departments and different disciplines. This is a creative enterprise. Who's up for this? Mix it up. Choose wisely and the next time around everyone is going to want in on the action: to be a member of the Big Idea Team, to do their bit!

The Best and the Brightest

In a large organization with entrenched silos, it's not going to be easy to assemble your team. There'll be push and pull the first time. Current managers will be unwilling to see their best people devoting a day (or more) a week on a project unrelated to their assigned role. Young hotshots will be eager to be on the team—and will be looking for self-promotion rather than the long-term viability of the business. The best people in the company will be unsure about whether joining the team is a good or a bad career move. They'll be thinking as much about their exposure to failure as they will about the possibility of success.

If you work for Google, you're invited to spend 20 percent of your time—the equivalent of one workday a week—tinkering with something you love, regardless of whether it has anything to do with the job you were hired for. In effect, Google has made their entire company a living, breathing, Big Idea model. So it's no wonder that Google seems to launch one revolutionary product after another, and has been growing virtually nonstop since it was founded. Imagine taking 20,000 of the best and brightest people in the software universe and telling them they have to spend one day a week working on something they're passionate about.

That's what you're trying to do with your Big Idea team. In essence:

- Collapse the layers.

- Get everyone on board.

- Get the team members fired up about what they're about to do.

Put together a mix. Young and old. Team players and odd ducks. Research and marketing. Finance and manufacturing. R&D and Sales. Interview possible players and tell them what you're planning to do. Watch their faces and their body language as you explain the idea to them. You'll know in a heartbeat who's wrong for the job. Probe a little deeper, and you'll discover who's right for the team.

Word to the Wise: Give careful consideration to either having a company lawyer on your Big Idea team or at least one on call as a part-time member, so you have someone to consult as things progress. This can save you a lot of problems and distress down the road. See Chapter 17, "Due Diligence," for an in-depth discussion of what attorneys will bring to the table.

Fire Up the Engines

PAUL TEACHES advertising at the college level. Every year a new crop of students comes into his introductory course. Today's students are all about social media. But when it comes to advertising, their knee-jerk reaction is that it's all about TV commercials, print ads, and billboards. So Paul starts the class with what he calls the new media quiz. It's about 30 questions long, covering everything from TV to texting to Tweeting and beyond, and asks them what media they use. Within the first 30 minutes of the semester, the expectations for how they should approach the subject matter for the next 14 weeks are dramatically altered. The quiz resets their mindset for consideration of a much wider world of advertising. It fires them up for a whole new look at advertising. And it sets the table for final advertising presentations that are out of the box and multiplatform.

Okay. You've got a green light. Congratulations. You've got your team. It's time to get to work. It's time to plan your team kickoff—a vitally important meeting that establishes the ground rules, the process, and the belief that you're going to be doing something special. It's the meeting that gets going the motivation that you are seeking to accomplish something extraordinary.

Just as your undertaking is not for the meek, neither is this meeting. Consider it carefully. It's a mission setter, but it's also a pep talk. You're the coach. You're getting the team fired up for the big game. The meeting will set the tone for all meetings that will follow. Where should you have the meeting? What time should the meeting be? Who should speak? What might you serve? What are you going to serve up? Location, timing, and speakers all have an impact on how the mission will be received and how jazzed the team will be for the upcoming endeavor.

Even though you've already got a team, you still need to do some formal investiture. This adds gravitas to everything the team will be doing. It sets the task in a manner that feels different, acts big, and generates excitement.

The War Room

Designate a war room. This is central command. It's a brand room where ideas flow all over the place. Four walls are best. Windowless is great. Have every wall tapeable, pasteable, stickable, writeable—you get the picture. Get a big white board in there for scribbles and scrawls, formulas, and formative ideas.

Get a room that can be locked, where even the cleaning people aren't allowed to enter. Start cleaning up your own mess and leave it outside the door. Too often we've heard horror stories about great ideas "walking out the door."

Bring in a file cabinet (or two) that also has a lock. Get in the habit of putting away work in progress that isn't attached to the wall at the end of each session.

Treat what you're doing with the utmost secrecy. Besides the obvious reasons—security, corporate theft, or simple tampering—many ideas will be fragile in their early stage. If anyone in the company can wander in and see what you're doing, you'll be amazed at the rumors that will spread and the way ideas—and possibly your team—can be killed before they have a chance to evolve and flourish.

Fill the room with competitive intelligence. Display competitive product and competitive advertising. Bring in other brands as live product and tear-outs of communications that benchmark ideas or areas of interest for your new discovery. A great logo, an inspired promotion, a terrific example of customer service. Make the room a motivating environment. This is where your innovation team will live and the place in which your innovation will be born!

Meet and Greet

A central fixture of your kick-off meeting will be first-meeting introductions. Even if everyone in the room knows each other, this task is a part of the process of reinvention. Have everyone introduce him- or herself. Have all participants add to their introductions some interesting fact (relevant to the task) about themselves, as well as making a personal statement about their specific interest in or planned contribution to the new initiative.

Think ahead about whether or not you want to have people prepare anything in advance of the meeting. Should they come with questions? Should they be given an advance assignment? Should you plan some sort of team-building exercise to kick off the meeting? The key is to have the tone and message of the meeting match the personality and process of the assignment ahead. Big and bold? Wise-ass and sassy? Personality matters.

New Possibilities Day One

Set the table for new possibilities. Make it clear that the "same old, same old" just won't do. This team has been hand-picked because you and management are confident that they're the people who can break the mold. Your team knows the rules. Now they get a chance to break those rules. You are fundamentally the optimist. The approach to this new assignment will be *Mission: Possible*.

You'll want to discuss what *possible* means. Great ideas require a suspension of disbelief, a willingness to follow blind alleys and go down rabbit holes through mystery to places of wonder. There will be a wide range of concepts to ponder and seeming nonsense that may ultimately make sense. Possible means perhaps.

The Rules for No Rules

We made a big deal about breaking the rules, but now it's time to set some. The first meeting has to lay the ground rules for the entire process. We're sure you'll have quite a few of your own, but here are just a few that in our minds are fundamental to the process:

1. *Secrecy:* Nobody—including spouses—should be told what's being developed. No exceptions. Maybe even have everyone sign a non-disclosure agreement (NDA). It serves as a further reminder that the stakes are high.

2. *Meeting schedules:* Determine how frequently, and for how long, you're going to meet. Once a week? Once a day? One weekend a month? Figure out what works for everyone and set the schedule. Everyone still has to do his or her normal job (unless you've sold in your idea so well that you've gotten release time for your designated team), so it can't be a full-time gig. Then make sure everyone agrees to the process, dates, meetings, and deliverables. No exceptions.

3. *Intranet:* Will the team have an Intranet setup? It should be password-protected and set up by your tech group so no one other than team members can access it. Once people start cooking ideas, there'll be a lot of digital back-and-forth outside the regular meeting times. Make sure this can be handled easily and securely.

4. *Two room keys:* No one is allowed in without signing in somewhere. Ditto the keys or combination to the file cabinet.

5. *No bad ideas:* In the initial development stage, no idea will be dismissed as too absurd, too risky, or too far afield. Good ideas are hard to come by and often come from what initially appears to be a bad one.

6. *Team changes:* You'll need a process for bringing on new players or part-time players or experts, as well as a means for letting some people go. Life happens. Sometimes you'll start exploring a new idea and realize that you don't have the right skill set in the room to fully develop that new idea. A process should be put into place to add or change team members, with no hard feelings or no bad marks on anyone's evaluation sheet.

7. *Team nickname:* We're fans of this. Builds esprit de corps. Have the group offer some suggestions. (If they can't even agree on a name for themselves, it might not bode well for future idea development.) Hey, people should be proud to be part of your company's skunkworks.

We're sure you'll have more rules and regs. Make a list, and make sure they make good sense. Then make covering these ground rules part of your first meeting.

Urgency

As we've said, there's no blank slate in the process of developing new products and services. You need to establish with your team both the pressure and the expectations for the project from the get-go. Management will want to see results from your efforts. You've worked hard to build in timetables and milestones for metrics. You need to share them with your team. They will all need to deliver as you have promised and planned.

"Business as usual" comes with a comfort factor built into it. Everyone knows the process and practice. Pursuit of the big new idea is different, however. The course is uncertain, and the road signs along the way need to be obvious. It's these road signs that hold management at bay and best ensure that they will fulfill their promise to give you the time and talent to complete your mission. But don't dawdle.

So right away, you've got to make some decisions: What are you going to explore, and in what time frame? We don't think your first meeting should be any kind of brainstorming session. It should be about meeting one another, getting to know each other's strengths and styles, and recognizing that you're all in this together. Team building.

Will you be meeting daily for an hour? Weekly for an afternoon? Do you want to treat this as a high school club (once a week after school for 90 minutes and then everyone catches the late bus home), or is it going to be an all-out push (one weekend day session every week until you've cracked it)? You should have done your own thinking about these questions before the first meeting, but now's the chance to discuss things with your team members to arrive at some sort of consensus. You don't want this to turn into the rigor of jury duty.

Roles Defined/Roles Undefined

You've selected your team carefully based on attitude and expertise. You likely have a range of disciplines represented. You want the roles clearly defined—R&D, creative, marketing, sales, whatever. But once the roles are established (and they're likely evident from the start), liberate every player from his or her expected discipline.

A team is always greater than the sum of its parts or, in this case, its prescribed roles. You're all in this together, and the idea is to land on something big rather than applauding individuals for their personal contributions. Everyone is going to work hard and pull his or her weight, or the person wouldn't be on the team. And, if there proves to be a single weak link, pull the individual from the team. You're only as strong as your weakest link.

In the advertising business, Bill Bernbach invented the idea of creative teams. It's common practice today—an art director and a copywriter working together as a team. After all, two heads are better than one. The two creative disciplines work together to land on bigger ideas, more fully conceived. It was a wildly innovative idea at the time. Putting copywriters and art directors together empowered a partnership of language and visual. It created an ongoing brainstorm of two minds. It made the creative process much less lonely and the output much richer. And in the best of teams, one often can't distinguish the writer from the artist. Both contribute and build upon each other's ideas—copy or art—to plant the small seeds that grow into big campaigns.

Flattening the Organization

A key move in your innovation team strategy is to remove the hierarchy. Don't have titles. Don't have a reporting structure, except for the team leader. Working through layers tends to compromise ideas. In the traditional management hierarchy, as ideas go up the ladder, everyone adds some input. For inspiring and building Big Ideas, that hierarchical process is counterproductive.

Paul vividly remembers—early in his advertising career—stewarding a commercial for Crest toothpaste. He was an eager young account executive at the time, diligently managing the process of copy revisions. With all client-level, legal, and network comments and approvals finally in, Paul took the storyboard—in draft 18—to his account supervisor and proudly proclaimed, "We have a commercial." Jim, his supervisor, casually said, without looking up, "No, we have an approved storyboard. We lost the commercial back around draft 8." It's a lesson Paul has never forgotten. Work that has to be reviewed, approved, and revised by a multiplicity of players will virtually always get blander, not better.

Designate a Scribe

It doesn't have to be the same person for the whole run. Rotate the job around the table, but make sure there is always someone taking notes at every session. We prefer doing it on PowerPoint rather than note paper or using Word. Using PowerPoint makes it easier to move pages around, organize the thoughts, and start to build what will eventually be the following:

1. Your record for the team

2. The presentation to management

3. The outline for your book (perhaps!)

The notes should be circulated among team members after each session so everyone can keep in mind what was discussed and what was agreed to. As you get deeper into the process, these notes are going to be an indispensable reference source.

. . . .

CASE IN POINT

Early on in the process that led to the creation of the Segway Personal Transporter (PT; the two-wheeled self-balancing electric vehicle), inventor Dean Kamen agreed to allow author Steve Kemper full access to the entire team and the entire development process. It didn't work out for various reasons, and Kemper was asked to leave before the project was revealed to the world. Kemper's book Code Name Ginger *is probably mandatory reading for you (and perhaps for your team as well), but it also raises an interesting point. Do you want to have a camera crew or author along for the ride? It's possible your team will do one of two things worth recording:*

1. Invent a breakthrough product or service. If you're the people who come up with clean, cheap, renewable energy, the world is going to want to know the story in detail.

2. Create a process you can market to other companies. It's possible your process will be so successful that you'll want to offer it to other companies. Having a detailed record of how you did it and how they can do it will be invaluable for monetizing your team's efforts and setting in motion the next Big Idea Team to find the next Big Idea.

· ·

With the introductions done, the framework agreed to, the note-taking duties assigned, the space and schedule all set, it's time to give out the first assignment. You can start right there, but we believe you should give everyone a chance to think about what you've just covered. So, for the following session, let 'em know what you want them to be thinking about—and let's get to work!

Parameters
and Process

PAUL WAS one of the four inventors of Hasbro's brand Transformers. The product was developed in Japan and had been launched in the United States under the name Diachron. It was initially advertised in tabletop demonstrations by a spokesman who turned the cars into robots and back into cars. They were three-dimensional puzzles for the kiddies. The product launch was an immediate and forgettable failure.

A couple of years later, Hasbro was presented with the opportunity to reconsider the product line for the U.S. marketplace. There were 14 products available: 6 cars, 1 truck, 6 planes, and a gun—all of which could be manipulated to turn into robots. That was the hand they were dealt. Those were the parameters. How do you make a product line out of that? The whole creative enterprise occurred in a car ride from Hasbro's headquarters in Pawtucket, Rhode Island, to New York City, a three-hour drive, with Paul's agency partners at Griffin Bacal, Tom Griffin and Joe Bacal, and Hasbro's head of marketing, Steve Schwartz.

The group had lots of experience in the toy business, so there were certain unspoken givens for a new line of toys for boys. What was going to be the dramatic hook for the product line? Who was going to be assigned the role of good guys and who would be the bad guys? What was going to be the plot line and the play pattern? The four-man team decided to make the cars the good guys and the truck their leader. Joe Bacal was quick to name them Autobots and Optimus Prime. The planes would be the bad guys with the gun their leader—Decepticons and Megatron. The story goes much deeper and the track record for the brand is now toy (and movie) legend. But the constraint of the existing products focused the invention of a language and a play pattern for the brand that has endured and prospered for over twenty-five years.

Parameters. It's one of those great words that suggest guidelines for proceeding without predetermining the creativity of the pursuit. Parameters are different from rules. They're not prescriptions for process. They're guideposts that enable a process to be more efficient.

There are two kinds of parameters you need to concern yourself with in the quest of your Big Idea:

1. What are your *team* parameters?

2. What are the *management* parameters?

Yeah, we warned you. There isn't an unlimited budget or unlimited patience in this process. Management will want to know what their best and brightest are up to.

Team Parameters

What's the process you're going to use? How much time and energy will your team expend to achieve your goal? What are the timings and milestones you'll be using to measure progress?

What's the definition of that result you're looking for? You need to determine what qualifies as a worthy end result of your process. What are the boundaries for the idea search? What will qualify as success? What will be looked at as anemic or too small to qualify as a Big Idea? These are the questions that help you set your parameters.

You need to set your guidelines well within a tight strategic framework. Because, as Norman Berry, head of creative at Ogilvy, used to say, "Give me the freedom of a tightly defined strategy." In the case of Transformers, the parameter was the product. The strategy and product idea, at least for year one, needed to be developed to embrace the 14 existing products. Ironically, in many ways, it made our job easier.

Another team parameter lies in the answer to the question, "What's the day job?" As we mentioned before, it's critical upfront to manage your resources, both in terms of your expectations and the team's, based on the sell to management. Is your team dedicated to this initiative for a period of time? Have they gotten released time from their "day jobs"? If so, you "own" them for a period of time and the specific deliverable. Terrific. If not, what percentage of each person's time do you have and how will you manage it relative to his or her ongoing responsibilities?

Management Parameters

Management parameters are an acknowledgment that you're on a leash. It may be a long leash, but you need to hold yourself responsible for the process and the results. What checkpoints along the way have you built into your process? What will be your reporting procedure? Who in management is your go-to person, your champion and protector? He or she is the person responsible for helping to manage the ongoing enthusiasm and continued support for your work, to keep management at bay and give you breathing room to do what you need to do.

Management Reporting

Setting the reporting structure and the expectations is critical in this process and involves four key steps. Depending on how ambitious the initiative is, these four steps may be repeated several times to ensure continued commitment via ongoing communication.

1. *Submissions.* What observations, findings, and ideas have you discovered along the way? How can you serve up your discovery in ways that are empowering to your team and meaningful to management?

2. *Dialogue.* What's the conversation, inside and outside the team engagement, that's going to advance your thinking without becoming an impediment to discovering something big? What can you share, and with whom, about the developing thinking, benchmarking, or ideation that might invite useful additional insights from resources outside of your team?

3. *Synthesis.* How can you get the best out of management to make your Big Ideas bigger—and better? You might start by considering a series of ideas that have been in the air for a while. Can you integrate them into a bigger, more elegant opportunity? Suddenly, it's an opportunity to bring those ideas to life (while maintaining a safe distance, in case it's a bust). If you strike the right note, there may be a sudden allocation of dollars.

4. *Consensus.* How will you get buy-in, both on your team and along the way, so that your Big Idea will be pre-sold when you bring it to the table at your final presentation?

Time and again we see vendors—especially advertising agencies—spring important work on their clients as if they were magicians pulling a rabbit from a hat. "Ta-Dah!" they exclaim. And they are amazed when the room doesn't respond with the same enthusiasm. The reason is that it takes time for a new idea to percolate and then catch peoples' enthusiasm. Especially if it's a groundbreaking new idea.

While you want to keep your work secret, as you develop new ideas you're going to want to "feel out" key people in management to sense how the idea will be received. It's always good, when you make a presentation, to have one or two allies in the room. In other words, take a lesson from the best trial attorneys. Treat management the way attorneys treat witnesses; never ask a question to which you don't already know the answer.

This is a delicate process, of course. Dissecting everything you are doing and putting it into frequent reports runs a very real risk of diluting both the creativity of the project and the grandness of the quest. And, it's a great disease in business today: Spending lots of time preparing management updates rather than driving the task at hand; that's small-time thinking and a big time-waster.

Scheduling and Presenting

Put it all into a schedule. What deliverables do you expect from your team and when? What do you plan to take to management and when? Who are the key players on your team for synthesizing and reporting information and providing updates? How will you present your insights? When? And, with what intended effect?

Remember, the best presentations are the ones that are so carefully planned that buy-in is virtually a foregone conclusion. You know the drill:

- Tell them what they're going to see.

- Tell them why it's inspired, brilliant, and so right for the business.

- Tell them why they're going to love it.

- Show them the idea.

- Review what they've just seen.

- Reiterate why it's so great—provide strong rationale.

- Remind them why they thought your idea is so strong.

- Invite comments (praise goes here).

- Outline the next steps based on all that wonderful enthusiasm you have built in to the presentation and let flow in the meeting.

Obviously not all of those points will be necessary to make in your interim reports. But you get the message. Take nothing for granted. At every step of your process, you've got to keep management informed. But, you've got to be equally vigilant because, at any time, you could be one step away from being canceled and disbanded. So, manage the enthusiasm at every turn and keep your options open.

Parameters Are Your Friends

To the extent that you're successful in setting and managing both team and management parameters, you'll be that much happier and more successful in managing your process. You want to avoid ever having to revert to process discussions in the pursuit of breakthrough ideas. Get that stuff out of the way, identified clearly and placed in the background of procedures, away from the inspiration. You've got a big mission. You don't want to be battling protocol and process as well.

STEP FOUR

Land on the Big Idea

9

What Are You Selling?

WHEN PAUL was a kid there was a store in a strip mall called The Hobby Shop. Paul frequented the store both on his own and on special walking trips with his grandfather. The Hobby Shop was full of toys and activities—kites, balls, art kits, just about anything that could be considered a toy-related hobby. No need to have a clever name or catchy positioning line. You saw a sign that said, "The Hobby Shop" and you knew what they sold. The proprietor knew what business he was in. So did his customers.

Fast-forward 35 years. Steve's kids are in middle school and there is a toy store in their hometown called The Age of

Reason, filled with all those "science toys" and hobbies that claim to make your kid smarter and more college ready. To the kids, it is still just a hobby shop, but the owner knows his real customers are the status-obsessed parents of those kids. The proprietor knows what business she is in. So do her customers.

Remember our earlier story of UPS? It became a breakthrough business success because they were grounded in the basics of the business. Or, as Steve so often likes to remind our younger creative people, "Never reject the obvious."

Inspired ideas and brilliant business practice are grounded in fundamentals. Being able to readily articulate the seemingly obvious is a critical dimension of the search for a new Big Idea. There's an excellent chance that a breakthrough idea lays hidden in a fundamental discussion of what business you're in and the many ways to leverage that business. So, a good place to start in the Big Idea ideation process is to focus on an understanding of what business you're in.

. . . .

CASE IN POINT

Jeff Bezos founded Amazon.com with a vision. Both the name of the business and the vision for it suggested that Bezos was interested in becoming a large and diversified online retailer. To the consuming public, the early assumption was that Amazon was an online bookstore. It was, initially. Made sense. Because in the early days of the Internet, people were wary about buying online. Besides the credit card security issues, people were concerned about ordering merchandise that they might not like when they received it. After all, they couldn't see, feel, or try it on. What if it didn't fit right? What if the colors weren't true to what was shown online? Would Amazon take it back? Would the consumer have to pay shipping twice?

Books—and later, music—made a ton of sense. You can't judge a book by its cover, or an album's content by its cover, so the experience of buying a book or music online came pretty close to that of buying such merchandise in-store. And with the ability to read book introductions or listen to 30 seconds of music tracks online, confidence in online purchases was advanced. There were no problems of color or fit. It was a great place to start a business called Amazon.com.

. . . .

Though an odd name for a book and music seller, Amazon made perfect sense for its founder's vision. Bezos's idea was to become a major and diverse e-tailer. And, that's exactly what Amazon has become. In its early days, before profitability but after expansion into music and electronics, Paul went to a business conference. The CFO of Amazon was one of the featured speakers. The audience was fascinated and a bit confused with descriptions of the expansion of the business beyond books and music. A question was put forward: "Is there any business you won't get into?" The CFO paused, smiled, and chuckled. It was a question she had certainly considered carefully, but likely not one that had been put to her in that way before. Her answer was simple and direct: "Water or concrete." There was nervous laughter in the room. Her response made clear what Amazon.com's business barriers were. In a business dependent on shipping, weight matters. It was to be Amazon's only limiter.

What Business Are You In?

We landed on this simple—almost patronizingly simple—question a couple of years ago. Time and again, we found the question, "What business are you in?" to be surprisingly—and somewhat painfully—relevant. In hundreds of speaking and consulting engagements, with a wide range of companies in diverse categories, we consistently have found that beyond the obvious (i.e., printing, banking, shipping), the precision of the business definition is lacking. The people in the business tend to commit one of two definitional sins:

1. They characterize their business in a generic way. We'll hear them say things like, "I'm an accountant." Or, "I'm an attorney." Well, so are tens of thousands of other people. And if you can't make the distinction in your own mind, how can you expect to do it in the minds of your customers or clients?

2. They believe they can do or be virtually anything they want to be. This completely ignores the question of "brand permission." That is, just because you want to do something doesn't mean your customers will give you permission. It's something you've got to earn by demonstrating your value to them.

Broad, generic, and lazy strategic thinking tends to make business practice sloppy as well. Employees are unclear about the vision or mission of the business, and priorities become moving targets that preclude efficiency, effectiveness, and job satisfaction. Not to speak of the myriad other questions, such as positioning, branding, target audience, sales, growth and paths to market, that need to be considered.

What Are You Selling?

Amazon's Jeff Bezos had a clear vision of what he was going to sell, right from the get-go. So much so that if he was going to be a major purveyor of books, he would also want to be a major seller of digital readers as the digital world evolves. Kindle anyone? Similarly, Steve Jobs knew the world wasn't waiting for just another MP3 player. His iTunes software delivered a closed system of music delivery to a cool new device that was fundamentally no better than other players out there. And today there are far more people who use iTunes than own iPods.

. . . .

CASE IN POINT

Coca-Cola is the world's most powerful brand. That doesn't mean that Coke can sell and do anything they want. This was a painful lesson for Coca-Cola apparel. Coke competes in the beverage business. They have the wisdom to understand that, now. But some years ago, Coke took a foray into the apparel business. Coca-Cola apparel was cool and desirable as a premium: Yeah, I'll wear a Coke shirt or a hat. But no one was going to build an entire wardrobe extolling and displaying brand Coke. The idea of getting into the fray with the Gap, Ralph Lauren Polo, or Abercrombie & Fitch just didn't make sense. A lot of money was spent opening upscale boutiques in various cities—only to find that the occasional T-shirt wearer didn't translate into a profitable apparel business model.

. . . .

Knowing what you're good at, committed to what it is you sell, is critical to the well-being of your company. It's just as critical to the pursuit of your next Big Idea or business extension. We hear horror stories all the time about new-product ideation sessions, and they usually go something like this:

The participants show up bright and early, ready and raring to go for a break in their everyday routine. This is going to be a creative day—for brainstorming, crazy-idea generation, with no right and wrong answers. The facilitator starts with a creative exercise to get the juices flowing. Throughout the day, there are other exercises and the wall of stickers fills up with tons of ideas, some wild, some intriguing. At the end of the day, everyone votes for their favorites. The facilitator cites the five or ten most popular ideas of the day and the session ends. Everyone leaves happy. What fun!

The next day, the brand manager sits at her desk with pads full of ideas and the five or ten selected concepts circled for further development. It gets very lonely. Inertia sets in, followed by paralysis. Because, in the clear light of today, yesterday's ideas are fun and fascinating, but they're mostly problematic. They're off strategy. They can't be manufactured. They'll be way too expensive. They don't have a ready-made distribution channel. And on and on. The bottom line? There is no bottom line because all the ideas are inconsistent with the business you're in.

What Are You Good At?

The Big Idea process has got to be strategically driven. So perhaps, as homework for your second meeting, you want to ask everyone to think about two simple questions:

- What business are we in?

- What are we good at?

Yes, in brainstorming there are no bad ideas. But brainstorming that isn't focused on a strategic template will likely produce no good ideas, either. Knowing clearly what you're good at—in the broadest relevant sense—will set the stage for better ideas that can be realized and can break through to big successes. Amazon.com = e-tailing—the biggest and best in the category. Pixar = CGI animation movies—the best stories with the best animation in the business.

Start by Analyzing Your Processes

A great starter exercise is to ask everyone to analyze every aspect of your business operation—and break the components down into the disparate parts. Do you have a fleet of trucks that deliver merchandise every day, and then return to the warehouse empty? Maybe those empty trucks could be turned into a secondary delivery business using computers and a business partner to figure out how to maximize that empty space on the return trip. Do you have a warehouse that's half-empty? Subdivide and rent out the unused space.

By the way, if you come up with these "small wins" as you're looking for your Big Idea, don't hesitate to share them with management. No reason your unit can't be showing a profit and displaying its value to the company long before you reach your ultimate objective. This analysis is probably the true meaning of out-of-the-box thinking. Take a look at your daily processes, actions that you take for granted, and explore fresh ways to turn those accepted practices into new revenue sources.

Printing brokers are independent sales representatives. They call on companies and solicit their printing business—usually representing two, three, or a half-dozen printers nationwide or around the world. While keynoting a regional convention of printing brokers, we heard a great story told by one of these representatives: He'd called on his largest customer and then asked to use the men's room on the way out, only to discover that it was out of toilet paper. When he asked his client if there was some, the client sheepishly explained that they hadn't had a chance to run out and pick some up.

This broker was smart enough to see a new sales opportunity—after all, what's the biggest part of the printing business? Paper! In a few minutes he'd worked out a deal with his client and now has a regular revenue stream supplying toilet paper and paper towels to the client's 14 plants and offices.

When we established PS Insights in 2006, we developed a clear business proposition: to simplify the complicated issues of business so they become actionable. We would work with companies to help them turn insights into Big Ideas that can be monetized in the marketplace. Once we landed on that positioning and established the strategy, it was easy to build a financial model from bottom to top.

Everything we do, from our tweets to our blogs, our booklets to our books, and our talks, lectures, workshops, and trainings, is about delivering clear, usable information and insights to companies large and small. Once we were clear about our goals and objectives, it was easy to look at all our intellectual property and determine whether it should be free (tweets, blogs) or available for a fee at different price points (webinars, booklets, books, workshops, consulting, etc.).

Every new idea we come up with for a book or a blog or a workshop has to meet the criteria we've outlined, and the criteria we've outlined also help us come up with ideas for books and blogs. It's a cycle that feeds itself.

What's Everyone's Elevator Speech?

Not only is it worthwhile spending time to focus on what you do and what you do best, it's also critical that everyone on your team share the vision. So start by challenging your newly assembled team to separately write down their "elevator speech" for your business. Then, have them all read their speeches out loud. Notice the amazing range of differences. These are the different perceptions of what your company's business is. You've got to get everyone in agreement on a clear, concise, differentiated, and defined elevator speech for your brand or business before you can even start. This is your common understanding, your baseline, your starting point. If everyone is all over the place in an understanding of who you are and what you do, your team will be working at cross purposes throughout the idea-development stage.

Is What You're Selling Worth the Investment?

Before you get too far down the innovation trail, there is a test of reasonableness you need to take. Is what you're selling worth the investment? You're going to spend a lot of time and energy coming up with a new Big Idea. The first question is, "Is the fundamental business you're in big enough and buoyant enough to float a new Big Idea?" There is some key business analysis you'll want to do here before unleashing your full creative power of innovation.

Sounds odd, but in truth, your team might come to the conclusion that the smartest thing to do would be to sell the company. Maybe you're so far behind the developmental curve that the cost to ramp up a competitive new product would just be prohibitive. In that case, your team is heading toward a cliff or brick wall at full speed.

Presumably you've done some—preferably much—of this work in selling the company's commitment to your innovation path. Assuming you have done this, it's time to tell and sell that vision to your team. If your work is incomplete here, though, complete it now. Don't go down the time-consuming and expensive path of Big Idea development if every member of your team doesn't believe that big results are possible. If there's an undercurrent of cynicism in the company's commitment and vision, now's the time to find out.

Benchmarking to Fuel Belief

After you've carefully and clearly defined the business you're in and identified what you do well, and also confirmed that the investment is worthwhile, get out of your category. Benchmark now to fuel greater belief. What businesses in what other categories do you and your team most admire? Write them down. Analyze the elements in the business idea that work so wonderfully well. Which of them are applicable to your business? Keep these business characteristics close by, because they will help you establish your own, customized criteria for success.

This is one of those "inspirational wall postings" we mentioned before. You might want to post articles, stories, or print ads about products, services, or other masterful ideas that can serve as benchmarks to help inspire your team. (Please, whatever you do, don't put up a set of those "inspirational" posters. They tend to produce noise and nausea rather than insights and innovation.)

. . . .
CASE IN POINT

Bonnie Hammer is CEO of USA Network. In the hugely competitive world of television, this network has evolved from what many cable networks are—a hodgepodge of undefined shows, some of which generate audience and most of which don't. Its tagline "Characters Welcome" is both a unifying identifier for its collection of shows and a strategic discipline for consideration of new shows. Every show idea is considered strategically in relation to at least three key attributes and is researched with audiences to prove that they deliver. As reported on Newsweek.com, July 2009, new shows are vetted and green-lighted based on the attributes of optimism, fun, and character centrism. From "Monk" to "Psych" to "Burn Notice" to "In Plain Sight" to "Royal Pains," the Hammer method has achieved an impressive track record of new "product" success.

To summarize, you've got to know who you are and where you are before you can decide where you want to go. Get your team together and spend the first meeting (or two) making sure everyone's on the same page regarding the business. Make sure they understand the current business situation and the opportunity this Big Idea will offer. Get everyone in alignment before you start wandering into the wilderness. Give everyone the freedom of a tightly defined strategy.

1.0

What Are You Looking For?

ONCE UPON a time, toothpaste was toothpaste. Usage was a matter of habit, and there was no particular reason to use one brand versus another. Except that's what your parents bought. It was the brand you grew up with. Colgate was the category leader—until Crest came along with a huge idea. What was Procter & Gamble's Big Idea? Add fluoride directly to the toothpaste. (This, in a time when freedom-loving Americans were still arguing about whether their local town should "poison" their water supply by adding fluoride to the water. It was a daring move by Crest.) Once P&G decided to take that step, they pushed it as far as they could. First, they got the American

Dental Association to endorse the new ingredient in Crest—and then they hammered their message home to every mom and kid in America with copy that, if you're over 45, you probably know by heart: "Crest has been shown to be an effective decay-preventing dentifrice that can be of significant value…."

That Big Idea rocketed Crest to the number one position in the toothpaste category by a factor of two—a 40 percent share to Colgate's 20 percent share of the market—until Colgate and other competitors added fluoride to close the market gap.

Once you focus on what business you're in and what you do best, you can turn your sights to finding new Big Idea(s) that will catapult your business ahead of the others. The first step is to identify what you're looking for. What will qualify as big enough? Is a new flavor a Big Idea? While a company like Kraft Foods might expect you to come up with that idea as part of your job description, it could require a Big Idea team at a smaller, less cutting-edge organization. Ditto for a new package or line extension. Unfortunately, we recognize that there are a lot of companies that don't do Big Idea thinking on a regular basis. For them, "green product or packaging" might constitute a Big Idea. And currently Marcal is making headway in the paper goods marketplace by staking out a green proposition, via its Small Steps products. But let's assume you're in the business of hunting bigger game—we hope much bigger game—like an ingredient that is proven effective in fighting tooth decay or a cure for cancer.

What Qualifies as "Big Enough"?

You want to start by identifying parameters for the Big Idea. What does that mean? Where will you hunt? What will you explore? What are the boundaries you want to operate within to uncover a game-changing innovation? Two suggestions, both of which will start to get your team's creative juices flowing, are:

1. *Draw a bull's-eye.* Start by putting your existing company model at the center of the target. Now, draw concentric circles out from the center and fill in what everyone thinks constitutes first-level ideas, second-level ideas, and so on. First-level ideas might be a half-price sale, a bonus pack, or a special promotion. A second-level idea might be refreshed packaging. You decide, but get the group thinking about different ways to extend the product/service/company from the simplest (cheapest) all the way out to the last level, which could be, "Build a rocket to colonize Mars." Hey, it's probably on NASA's list—what would be your version of a Mars Mission?

2. *Draw a strategic map (x/y two-axis strategic grid).* Set your axis attributes that are meaningful both within your category and expansive for your new idea quest. Bottom to top might be cost, from cheap to expensive. Left to right might be conventional use to life changing. Use any attributes that will advance your thinking—and feel free to come at this exercise by playing with attribute variations to land on different ideas and platforms. As you do this exercise, you'll get everyone's creative juices flowing while mapping different strategic arenas for fruitful exploration.

Start by Failing

Challenge the team to come up with ideas that are likely problematic—that could be big failures. You'll be amazed at how liberating that assignment is. Granting permission to fail is a vitally important piece of the innovation process. By definition, if you're looking for something big, you may uncover something so radical, so in front of its time, that it may fail. Consumers may not "get it." The utility of the new idea may need to be taught.

A new idea may fail because consumers are just not yet ready for it or don't yet understand how it fits into their lives. That doesn't make it a bad idea. It just may mean that this is an idea before its time. Or it's an idea that requires a special communication for consumers to take it up. But without granting the team permission to fail, ideation will stay safe. Innovation will focus on items and ideas that are close at hand, readily understood by everyone, useful but small.

You can and should do that kind of out-of-the-box thinking in your regular day job (even if you don't share your big ill-conceived ideas with anyone). But often, ideas that seem destined to failure can be turned, spun, and piggy-backed to become compelling opportunities for success. It just takes a little work—and rework.

Paul has an exercise he does with his students to come up with a compelling idea to sell umbrellas on campus on a beautiful sunny day. In one class, a student suggested leveraging the benefit that umbrellas will protect you from the sun. College students believe they are invincible, so the idea was roundly rejected by everyone present. Another student piggy-backed on the idea, suggesting that the umbrellas could be designed with an appropriate logo and dedicated to research on skin-cancer prevention. The students, being "cause sensitive," embraced this idea as a good premise for selling the umbrellas. This selling proposition was particularly relevant on a bright, sunny day—a simple "repositioning" turned the rejected idea into a winner.

Permission to fail is an invitation to think big, to become unfettered by traditional answers and classic formulas—in product, in market, in management. And failure is often our best teacher. We ask ourselves, "What did we put out there?" "Why didn't it get picked up?" "What have we learned?" "If we did it again, what would we do differently?"

. . . .

CASE IN POINT

Procter & Gamble (P&G) is consistently cited as the company that invented modern marketing. Their new-products model was so well honed that for a short while in the 1990s it became a bit of an impediment to the kind of success they'd traditionally enjoyed. In the digital era, the idea of a classic test market, with traditional media in carefully matched markets, became both an unaffordable luxury and a competitive disadvantage.

P&G has largely reinvented its entrepreneurship and marketing methods over the past decade by exploring new ranges of marketing, investing in new businesses, and divesting itself of slower or poorer performing brands and categories. P&G pioneered the soap business and markets the number one laundry detergent, Tide. We've been watching a fascinating new initiative (as of this writing) from P&G–Swash. (We could tell you where to find their test site, but we're feeling magnanimous and don't want to screw up P&G's test model by sending a whole bunch of nonusers to the site.) Swash is a diverse line of apparel-care products that capitalizes on the equity of Tide for cleaning clothes. The four Swash products actually don't clean at all. Targeted to college students and 20-somethings, they are convenience products that smooth, freshen, steam, and remove stains from clothes to make them wearable without washing.

When you enter the Web site, P&G asks if you would be will-
ing to answer a simple four-question questionnaire upon
exiting the site. Very clever. Very low-cost. Totally viral. As of this
writing, virtually no one we've spoken to knows what's going
on. But we've become ambassadors for the brand by taking
people to the site in many of the talks we give. Yes, there is a
real, live in-market test in Lexington, Kentucky. But the learning
P&G can get from the digital play of this new brand not only
represents fabulous innovation but also inspired go-to-market
research and media testing.

The idea that Tide would "parent" products that don't actually clean had to be viewed as pretty revolutionary initially. It all
relates to how you define the product category you're in. "Tide
knows fabrics best" is the brand line that will greet you at
Tide.com. It suggests that the world of Tide has moved far
beyond washing clothes in a washing machine. It's a position
that the brand has permission to venture into. Long-established
credentials in cleaning give Tide the opportunity to seek extensions beyond the washing machine.

Yet it's quite likely that some of the innovations on their
Web site might fail. Consumers get to vote online, through the
mail, and ultimately in the market to support these new ideas.
Some may become big business additions to the Tide franchise.
Some may simply disappear. It's clear in the Tide pantheon of
the twenty-first century that failure is not just an option, it's
also built into the DNA of an expanding brand.

So, the value of writing a "let's fail" scenario is that the germ
of a great idea might be out there. In effect, you've been a sneak
and gotten your team to do some creative ideation without

telling them they have to come up with the Big Idea. Everyone's having fun thinking of guaranteed failures. Once you've all had a good laugh, and have generated a good list of wild ideas, challenge the group to identify why each of those ideas would fail—and how they could turn them into winners. And don't be surprised if from the ashes of your stated failures you come up with a Big Idea right there!

No Risk, No Reward

The game is "no risk, no reward." Often spoken, seldom practiced. Your team is built for this game. Risk is the way forward.

Think baseball. It's a tied game, bottom of the ninth, with no one on. You're swinging for the fences. Your goal is the walk-off home run. Boy, does that feel great. The more frequent strikeout, however, is neither the end of the game nor the end of the world. You're going into extra innings. There will be more at-bats.

Singles and doubles are the stuff of everyday work. The towering long ball is what you're aiming for. So, again, redouble your setting of the parameters. What are you seeking? What will qualify as that towering hit?

. . . .
CASE IN POINT

Procter & Gamble (P&G) pioneered the disposable diaper. Convenience seemed like a good idea at the time. But, it took Pampers a number of failed launches before P&G took the diaper industry by storm, leading to the virtual demise of cloth diapers and diaper cleaning services. The company could have easily packed up and "gone home." The paradigm of baby care was cloth diapers.

WHAT ARE YOU LOOKING FOR? **103**

Several failed efforts cost P&G major investments in trying to
crack the code. Cost per diaper was an issue. So was conven-
ience and disposability. Learning from each failed attempt was
critical. And, ultimately, the benefit proposition had very little to
do with mom (and everything *to do with mom). The ultimate*
and winning insight was that it was all about baby. The motiva-
tion for buying Pampers—relative to cloth diapers—became that
of having dryer, more comfortable babies. The disposable
diaper transformed infant care in America and built an entirely
new category.

Too Soon for "No"

P&G not only had deep pockets, they also had deep patience, conviction, and persistence. With Pampers, they understood that creating a new business would be time-consuming—and it also had to be consumer-changing. Pampers was about replacing a classic tradition in baby care, cloth diapers, with "convenient, paper, disposable diapers."

This is our reminder that whatever ideas you come up with at this point in the process, it's *way too soon* for either yes or no. Your innovation team has been vetted because you are opti- mists, risk takers, and resilient. You don't want to take no for an answer. And you don't want to jump on the first clever thought and say, "Well, we're done." Everything should be written down, added to the pile, put aside, and then reconsid- ered at a later date. Meanwhile, keep moving on. There are many more ideas you'll want to consider before landing on your behemoth business changer.

Changing Taste, Changing Behavior

What's going on out there? Are people's tastes shifting? You betcha. And one way to look for a Big Idea is to build on the inspiration of a solution to a behavior. Can you come up with a new product or service that makes sense as an alternative to current behavior? Or, is the new product or service so revolutionary that it becomes an entirely new way of navigating one's way though life? Did someone say GPS?

· ·

CASE IN POINT

SONY lost its way in the late 1990s because it lost touch with changing consumer tastes. As recently as 15 years ago, we all walked around with Walkman CD players, which had replaced Walkman cassette players. They were the branded gold standard in portable music players. But SONY looked at MP3 and didn't want to play. As a technologically driven company, they were dismissive of the audio quality available on MP3. So they ignored the technology—and Apple waltzed right in. Hmm. Same thing happened to them when VHS beat their superior Betamax video product for mass consumer usage.

· ·

Take a look at consumer tastes. Always follow the trends. Read, study, go online. Build into your company and your team the mechanisms to be up-to-the-minute with consumer behaviors and desires. As company policy, you know that the customers are always right—but they might not always be visionary. Your great idea may need to be spoon-fed or explained in a way that establishes a benefit proposition that finally resonates. More often than not, you'll be launching an idea into a marketplace that is not hungry for your innovation—until you make it clear how incredibly useful your innovation is. Until then, the market is satisfied with what's out there.

. . . .

CASE IN POINT

Procter & Gamble (P&G) again. Yeah, they're that good. Potato chips. The world was certainly not waiting for a new form of potato chip. There are well over 100 different potato chip brands in the United States. There are the national players and lots and lots of proud local brands that satisfy consumers with their great taste, flavor, crunch—whatever. Into this crowded happy marketplace P&G decided to launch a convenient chip, a reconstituted chip, a stackable chip. Enter Pringles—uniform chips in a tennis can-like canister.

The world did not run to the Pringles door. Taste is the high ground in snack food consumption, with growing credentials for texture in the chip category. Pringles delivered well on neither of these high-ground benefits. P&G would not take no for an answer. They went back and reformulated. Taste was improved. So was texture. Convenience was built into the essential form of the brand. Parity or close to it in taste and texture to regular chips, with the added benefit of convenience, proved a winning combination. Now, very strong national brand garners more customer "facings" than any of its competitors. Retailers can display more packages and a wider variety of types of Pringles because of its compact packaging.

. . . .

So, start with what you know and build out from there. Keep the ideas coming—even ones that won't work. Keep looking for new trends, new tastes, and new ways to connect with your customers. Don't be afraid to take risks because big risks can lead to big rewards.

The Competitive Landscape

ONCE UPON a time, when we were young and foolish, we were on a softball team together. New York City runs numerous leagues all summer long, and we both worked for ad agencies that didn't field teams. So we formed a ragtag assortment of unaffiliated players. The team wasn't very good, and in the spirit of the times, we named ourselves "Brand X." We had a good laugh when we came up with that name.

Whenever we showed up for a game, the opposition knew they were playing Brand X. Brand X (back in those days, when you didn't mention the competition) was, in the parlance of the ad business, the loser product that would always get beaten in the end. Which is what happened to us just about all summer long. Virtually every team we faced expected to beat us and most did. Plus, nobody wanted to lose to Brand X. We fulfilled the prophecy of our name! That was an interesting life lesson about "What's in a name?" and "Raise your expectations."

Now that you've spent time (a session? a week? a month? Take as long as you need, as long as it's in line with your timeline) sifting through your company's existing situation for Big Idea inspiration, it's time to look next door: What's your competitive landscape?

A key way of defining what business you're in, what you do well, and what you offer that's unique and meaningful is to identify your competitive landscape. There are lots of ways to land on Big Ideas, but a critical dimension of vetting the Big Idea is to understand where it fits and how it's likely to perform within a competitive framework.

Close-in Competition/What Category Are You In?

A first step is the obvious exercise of identifying the product or service category in which you operate. It's got to be broad, it's got to be meaningful, but at the same time it's got to be specific. No one is in the "television business," for example. Do you manufacture flat-screen TVs? Do you develop TV programming? Are you a scriptwriter? Are you in the TV ad sales business?

Even with those parsed categories within the TV business, what specifically do you do? And who are your biggest competitors? Are you a comedy writer or an action/adventure writer? Do you do local ad sales or national ad sales? First, you've got to tightly define your business; then you identify your three to five (probably at most) serious competitors. In fact, if you can list more than a half-dozen serious competitors, you haven't tightly defined your business.

Do this as a team exercise. Get everyone to agree on who the key competitors are. You need to be able to characterize your competitors and understand them very well in order to effectively compete with them—or come up with a Big Idea that will leapfrog those key competitors. Once you've identified them, start compiling a list of things they do better than you that you could do as well—or better!

Competition Beyond the Competition

There's another class of competition out there that is also critically important to understand. What are the other barriers that may preclude your business or new Big Idea from gaining traction? What else is out there that matters? What's on the horizon that could matter? Is it a new competitor? A new technology? A new media platform?

- -

CASE IN POINT

Dunkin' Donuts did a good job of fighting off the meteoric rise (and decline) of Krispy Kreme Doughnuts. At the same time, they had to fight the coffee wars with Starbucks, McDonald's, and others. But as of this writing, there's a new threat on the horizon. Canada's number one doughnut chain, Tim Hortons, just took over nine Dunkin' Donuts stores in the United States. Ouch. A completely new source of competitive pressure in the United States that Dunkin' Donuts has to keep an eye on in order to maintain their share of the market.

- -

Is there a new economic pressure that's going to force you to respond? How about $5 Footlongs from Subway forced everyone to play a price game in the sandwich business. The tough economy seriously (and possibly permanently) altered family restaurant behavior. The under $20 dinner for two wasn't a happy innovation for these restaurants, but it was a survival response to the tough competitive pressures forcing sharp pricing reductions to fill tables. You've got to look at what's coming down the road and be ready to respond.

War Room (Take 2)

You've set up your war room. Here's an important way to use it well and have it as headquarters for all your go-forward work.

Dedicate at least one wall to competition. Have live product. Post pictures of product lines and price points. Include competitive factors further afield, but be sure to include real barriers to your mission beyond the close-in-category threats. These barriers are the villains—the enemy or potential enemies. How will your Big Idea neutralize them—or better, vanquish them? The war room keeps all the competitive players on center stage, in your face and peering at you at all times, challenging you to deal with them.

What's a Good Idea Worth?

All ideas are not created equal. Some ideas will inherently be bigger than others. But as you look at the competitive landscape, you might stumble on major incremental sales and profit opportunities without commensurate effort. This might be a smart thing to put in front of management as if to say, "See? We're paying you dividends already."

. . . .

CASE IN POINT

The coffee business was in long-term decline until Starbucks came along. Maxwell House (from Kraft Foods) and Folgers (then, from P&G) were battling it out with two crusty, old spokeswomen—Cora and Mrs. Olsen—extolling the virtues of their brands at the expense of the other. The advertising neither celebrated the coffee category nor tempted the young consumers who were drinking Coke and other caffeine alternatives to start their day.

Both businesses got wisdom when they changed campaigns in an effort to stem declines in coffee consumption and celebrated coffee in general and their brand differentiation in particular. Maxwell House ran "Good to the Last Drop," demonstrating people enjoying coffee at all times of day for stimulation, relaxation, and sociability. Folgers took ownership of the morning with "The best part of waking up is Folgers in your cup." It helped, a little.

But it wasn't until Starbucks came along that the coffee business got a real jolt and started to grow. Starbucks celebrated the coffee experience in a coffeehouse environment. The smell of the beans, the preparation of coffee by baristas, the candied confections called Frappuccinos. A new generation of coffee drinkers signed on to the Starbucks experience. Supermarket coffee brands further eroded.

Well, if you can't beat 'em, join 'em. And an inspired but unlikely hook-up, a true frenemy play (before the term came into use), meaning a competitor who can also become a collaborator, took place when Kraft Foods became the supermarket distributor for Starbucks. What an easy alliance. Kraft was already in the supermarket sales business, distributing Maxwell

House. Carrying another coffee brand—and a very desirable one, at that—was no problem. An easy sell-in, incremental sales and easy additional profits.

Where Do You Get a Good Idea?

The preceding case study suggests that good ideas are everywhere. Beyond the realm of idea generation (to be discussed in detail in the next chapter), good ideas are out there. Look to your competitors and the wider world of your competitive barriers for keys to new inspiration. You may be able to work with them, work around them, or come at them. It's virtually never a good idea to be number two on the same idea. But, success can lead to other successes built on the same idea. Starbucks at retail is a good business.

How to Recognize and Nurture Success

When you see a winning idea, go for it. Benchmarking the successes of the wider world of competition surrounding you can offer terrific inspiration for your own new initiatives. The key is to observe well, identify the winning elements of the competitive initiative, and tailor your own program to be strategically consistent with your brand on your terms.

CASE IN POINT

The fast-food chains have drunk from the golden fountain of coffee. This product is now a high-interest, high-margin category. Coffee draws people into stores in the morning. McDonald's, a company that spent a lot of time, energy, and money developing their breakfast daypart, saw the opportunity of stepping up their game in coffee. So did their competitors—Burger King and Wendy's. Premium coffee has become the new high ground everywhere. But McDonald's has taken it a step further. McCafés have been around for years—a more active branding proposition around the world than in the United States. But the McCafé idea completely delivers on the promise of coffee done well and done in a number of recipes. McDonald's has now stepped up its game in the coffee wars to build added attraction to the morning and throughout the day as a purveyor of designer coffee. They're even the sponsoring coffee of Fashion Week in New York City. Talk about high end.

• •

Okay, you've mined your existing situation. You've mined the competitive landscape. We hope you've got at least a dozen viable ideas already. But regardless of the number, it's time to take off into the wild, blue yonder of ideation.

Coming Up with the Big Idea

THE NINETEENTH-CENTURY mathematician/philosopher Henri Poincaré once described how he came up with the solution to a problem he'd been struggling with for months. Shut behind his office door, and with piles of paper before him, he'd failed to come up with the proof he was seeking. Finally, he left his office and went for a stroll, determined not to think about the idea. As he recounted the story, just at the moment he placed his foot on the first stair of the bus, the entire proof flooded into his mind. In a Eureka! moment, he saw the entire solution, elegant and complete.

Isn't that a cool story? We thought so, too. But how many times has that happened to you? Totally frustrated, you get up from your workspace and stroll down the hall for a cup of coffee. And suddenly, on the way to the soda machine, the entire solution just pops into your head.

What we're trying to tell you is that once you decide you're *looking* for good ideas or new ideas, they *will* just start coming to you. Once you dedicate an entire team of people to focusing on and finding fresh ideas, you'll experience a river of new thinking. Yeah, we know, that sounds a little airy-fairy. But the simple truth is that it works. And if you want the science behind the theory, you can either read Malcolm Gladwell's book *Blink* or Henri Poincaré's book *Science and Hypothesis*, in which he explores the way the mind makes unusual or unexpected connections.

Idea Generation

Idea generation takes many forms; but this book is not focused on the dynamics of ideation. You'll find dozens of books on the shelves that can give you various techniques for finding and generating ideas. What we're giving you here is a clinic on how to take great ideas and use discipline to build them, protect them, and make them happen—in the marketplace, where they count.

But here's our critical piece of idea advice: *relax*. You've already got more ideas than you can handle. You just don't know that you've already got them. Don't underestimate the power of your subconscious or unconscious. Once your mind knows it's supposed to be working on a paradigm-busting problem, it will put numerous ideas in front of you. They'll come to you in the shower. On the way to work. Listening to your iPod.

Humming a song. Walking through the mall. Playing with the kids. Jogging. Drinking. Daydreaming. Night dreaming. Just about anywhere, anytime.

You won't know when ideas will hit you, but they will. So keep a pad and pen or a PDA handy. Write down the idea, text yourself, or call and leave yourself a message outlining your idea. Because your ideas—like dreams—will often flee as fast as they arrive, and if you don't record them they'll be gone. Don't blame us. We warned you. One of the many advantages we have in working together is that Steve is forever capturing Paul's ideas and writing them down. And Paul captures Steve's ideas. We often say to each other, "Did you write that down?"

So even though idea generation isn't the mother lode of this book, let's talk about some of the many ways you can come up with ideas for new products, services, features, benefits, and competitive advantages—whatever you set your mind to do!

Put the Company to Work

We'll make you a guaranteed bet (if we're right, just send us a $100 check in the mail—and we know we're right on this one): at least one person in your company already has a terrific idea for your brand, your business, or your company, but just doesn't know who to tell it to or how to benefit from it.

Really.

Remember when you first started working in business, and you were wondering why the company you worked for wasn't doing things in a different way? Or, why they weren't manufacturing X product? Your organization is filled with people who have bright ideas and have no means to give them to anyone. The corporate culture doesn't invite them. It isn't part of the job description. It's too risky. Whatever.

So, for openers, give everyone the opportunity to have a good idea. Encourage creative thinking. Reward it. Provide a clear method for people to have an outlet for their ideas. It could be as simple as the classic suggestion box. But it could and should go a lot further than that. The good ideas you can garner from your own people will virtually always be the least expensive investment you can make in positive change.

We had a friend who spent her entire career as an idea generator in the fragrance business. And it's a lot harder job than you can imagine. Okay, well, a hell of a lot easier than digging trenches, we'll grant you that.

She started out as a salaried employee. Then, she became a senior manager with an incredible salary. Then, she negotiated ridiculous bonuses for each one of her ideas that went to market. Eventually, her last deal gave her a percentage of the gross cost of ingredients—for life—for every fragrance that went to market. We're talking a tiny percentage—less than 1 percent—but that's about every single bottle of each fragrance sold! (For a small fee, we'll give you the name of the attorney who negotiated that deal!)

Rewards and Incentives

You don't have to be nearly so generous as the fragrance story suggests, but you should definitely put into place some kind of reward structure for your employees and teammates. Let the entire company know there's a new product team in place. Then, let them know you'll gladly welcome all ideas. And let them know you're paying:

- Some gift or money order or cash card for every idea submitted

- A larger dollar amount for every idea considered

- A significant bonus for any idea that goes to market

And as you develop the budget for the implementation, test, and launch of your Big Idea, you should probably build in some kind of bonus incentive for your development team members for any idea that makes it to market.

You'll be amazed at the flood of ideas that will come in. And you'll also be impressed with the kind of thinking that's going on all the time within your organization.

Steve has three patents to his name. But he knows he's an idea man, not a product-development person. So whenever he comes up with a patentable idea, he contacts a patent-development company he works with and negotiates a deal that gives them between 95 and 98 percent of the rights to the invention. Steve's philosophy is, "I'd rather have one percent of something than a hundred percent of nothing." (Paul is challenging Steve on the percentages he gives away.) But Steve knows that having the idea is really just a small step in the overall process, and he's more than willing to give away most of the revenue in return for someone else's talents, investment, money, and expertise.

. . . .
CASE IN POINT

Way back in the 1980s, John Hendricks came up with the idea for the Discovery Channel. Over the years, as the network grew and the opportunity arose to acquire or launch additional net-works, Hendricks gave away percentages of ownership in return for other peoples' skills. Today, he owns a very small stake in Discovery Communications—but it's a company that's worth *something north of $30 billion. So what would you rather have? A hundred percent of a million-dollar company or, say, 2 percent of a $30 billion company? We'll save you the trouble on the math. That second number is $600,000,000.*

How to Get Ideas—Let Me Count the Ways

We've already established that ideas are everywhere and resident with everyone. So here's the fun part. You started your idea team because you believed there was something bigger, newer, more profitable to bring to your business. Now, bring them together and start mining their knowledge, skills, and expertise for those ideas.

Brainstorming

The most common form of ideation is brainstorming. It's a great tool and it comes in many "flavors." There are lots of ways to provide the stimulus for brainstorming ideas. But brainstorming is also one of the most misused ideation processes out there. In fact, a high percentage of brainstorming sessions we've witnessed over the years don't work—either they become blamestorming sessions or they are brainhording sessions. Both are hugely unproductive. Blamestorming occurs when people spend their time blaming other people in the room for the reasons an idea won't work. Brainhording occurs when people suddenly have great ideas but keep the ideas to themselves so they don't have to share credit or have the idea taken away from them. We hope that the Big Idea team you've developed is way beyond those petty traps in ideation.

Another major problem with brainstorming is the treatise that "no idea is a bad idea." Not true. Many of the ideas offered up in a brainstorming session will be dumb, terrible ideas. The brainstorming process should encourage all kinds of ideas. But it shouldn't end without a critical filter to eliminate the bad ideas and cultivate the good ideas.

So, if you're going to do a brainstorming session, be clear about its structure and purpose:

1. *Invite the entire team.* Make it clear that the session is part of the team's development program. You can have just one at the beginning or (our preference) schedule them at regular intervals.

2. *Have a plan.* Read *The Little Blue Book of Marketing* by Paul Kurnit and Steve Lance (in our experience, two brilliant marketers). It's a guide to running a structured idea session. Use the structure of the planning session outlined in that book to guide the brainstorming session. You should have specific objectives, purpose, and structure to the meeting. Otherwise, a brainstorming session will just spiral out of control.

3. *Have toys and food in the session.* Toys (literally) signal that you're inviting everyone to play. Food is the fuel that keeps their minds focused. Make sure you've got both.

4. *Have a facilitator.* Choose someone who can be a member of your team, and prepare the individual with a wide range of relevant stimuli. Here's where you can pick up any number of ideation books and adopt and adapt blue-sky thinking exercises for your purposes.

Some of the exercises we like included in a brainstorming session are:

- *Ordinary Objects.* Pick up any object lying around your office. Ask everyone to think of a new use for the object. Or ask them to think of a line extension. Now, do that to your own products or services.

- *Word Association.* Grab a newspaper, magazine, or book, and have each person, in turn, randomly pick a word from it. Now, have everyone use that word to develop a new idea.

- *Positive Associations.* Favorite holiday locations, loved foods, best teachers, must-have Web sites—what are the elements of these favorites that represent fuel for your new idea? How can they be designed, adopted, and adapted for your brand?

- *Borrowed Items.* Take your benchmarking work to heart and identify as a group the best brands, businesses, management, processes, and people out there. Go beyond your category. Why do you admire them? What characteristics of these "best of" can you borrow and apply for your Big Idea?

- *The World As It Isn't.* Ask one person to pick some aspect, product, or feature of the world as it is today—and change the world by removing it. ("What if our world had no cars?" "What if there was no gravity?" "What if there were no elevators?" What if there were no cell phones?") Now, have everyone start to describe how the world we know it would be different. And how could they circumvent those differences to fulfill the need vacated by the removed element? First, have them look through those differences for new product ideas; then, have them apply the same technique to your own business. What would the world look like if your leading competitor didn't exist? What if your business category had not yet been invented?

• *Worst to Best.* Have everyone in the room try to think of the worst possible new idea you can imagine for your company. As bad as possible. Like vomit-flavored chewing gum. Or 30-pound running shoes with no arch support. Bad as you can imagine—and then even worse. Make sure everyone enjoys this one and has a good laugh. Once you've got a number of terrible ideas, break the team up into groups of three or four and have each group try to turn each bad idea into a good idea—to find the 180-degree idea that might be worth considering. So the 30-pound running shoes with no arch support might become an extraordinarily durable pair of running shoes that only weigh 3 ounces. You'd be amazed at how many good ideas will come out of having the bad ideas first.

• *Think About the Unthinkable.* Go specifically where you believe the company will never let you go. If you're working for a green-energy wind-turbine manufacturer, bring up the idea of manufacturing nuclear power plants. In other words, stick a spear through the company's sacred cow and see what happens. Tromping all over the company's sacred ground can often lead to breakthrough ideas and innovations. Go ahead and smash those sacred cows. The company has always done certain things specific ways. What if you changed the rules? Altered the religion? Set up a new set of beliefs and processes? Where would you go? What would you do? And what insights and ideas does that suggest?

Divine Intervention

We could go on and on with the dynamics of ideation. All ground is fertile. All stimuli are fair game. Be open. Understand that Big Ideas fall from the sky or show up in your morning shower all the time. Be on the lookout for them. Be open to them. Be receptive to them.

Finally, never dismiss the power of prayer. If you are by nature a religious person, ask your God to send you an idea. Chances are, she will.

13

Give Every Idea
a Chance to Live

IT TOOK NEARLY two years and many, many people to come up with the tag line "Explore Your World" for the Discovery Channel. The irony is that it was there sooner than anyone thought—they just didn't see it.

Through a series of focus groups, marketing exploratories, brainstorming sessions, and testing, it was clear that Discovery viewers were more than just couch potatoes. They felt actively engaged in the experience. At first, many of the lines ("Get This Close") were about Discovery, but gradually they moved more and more toward the promise of the audience experience.

When the line "Explore Your World" appeared in a focus group session, everyone knew it the minute they heard it. But when we went back and checked our notes, we found that the line had been offered up twice before—as long as a year before the line was "discovered." The problem was that it was buried in a batch of other lines. It hadn't been given the proper space to live, breathe, and come to life.

As you move forward with your strategic development, you've got to start making choices. But rather than just dismiss ideas out of hand, now's the time to start delving deeper into everything you've already got.

Another Day, Another Process

Don't try to come up with a breakthrough idea in a single, two-hour meeting or a half-day session. After you've conceived a number of ideas, take some time and let them all percolate, brew, simmer, and age. Don't be in a rush to get it all solved in a single afternoon. Ideas are precious. Circulate the list of ideas among your development team and let them all think about the list for at least a week, maybe more. Then when you're ready to meet again, review every idea—good and bad.

The place to start is with a sharpener, not pruning shears. Bring the team together and see how the ideas have "worn." Which ideas do people have continuing energy and enthusiasm for? How many variations of the ideas can you find in the ideas you've come up with? Look over the entire list. And, working together as a team or in groups, develop variations, alternatives, and any new ideas to what should already be a rather robust list.

Let's say someone had the idea of "micro stores" in your session. Great! But take it a step further. What about pop-up stores? Mall kiosks? Or the elaborate, Japanese-style vending machines that we've seen at airports, from which you can buy anything Best Buy sells that a traveler could need. Every idea you've got on your list can probably spark four or five variations, additions, or refinements.

Do this elaboration of ideas while the enthusiasm is still there. And if you can't find a variation for an idea, don't discard the idea. Give yourself some time to mull it over and see if it could be a winner all by itself.

· ·
CASE IN POINT

Coffee purists like their coffee straight: that is, with or without milk or sugar—but not flavored! Yet, research indicated that people were interested in flavored coffees. Conventional wisdom indicated that one of the major coffee brands might come out with a line of flavored coffees. Nestlé, already a big player in global coffee, took another tack. Today, Coffee-mate comes in numerous forms and flavors. It's not coffee at all. But it's the perfect additive for the noncoffee drinker who likes coffee with that flavorful confectionery taste.

Or, consider the growth of Google. They did one thing extraordinarily well: search. (Or, as Paul likes to say, find.) Great start. But then they took all the expertise they had in-house and began to ask themselves a different set of questions. Not, "How can we do search better?" But, "What can we offer consumers if the world truly is moving to mobile-platform computing?" The result is an extraordinary array of features and services—and now they've taken on the 500-pound gorilla directly by launching their own Web-oriented operating system. Sure, that may not have been in their original business plan, but that's the hallmark of a company that thinks big.
· ·

But back to work. Yeah, we mean you.

Take a look at your list and find the ideas that are the most out of the box. Then, instead of crossing them off, ask yourself whether your customers will give you brand permission to do them.

. . . .

CASE IN POINT

Time and again, for the first 20 years of its existence, pundits would write about the impending death of Apple Computer. But the Apple people never felt constrained in being an exclusively computer company. They are a consumer-centric technology innovation company. So Apple completely revolutionized the music business when they saw an industry in disarray—and an opportunity to create iTunes and iPods.

Then Apple completely revolutionized the smart-phone business by not only introducing the iPhone but also the whole idea of applications (apps). And along the way, they changed the company name from Apple Computer to Apple Inc. What will they innovate next? No one knows—because consumers give Apple enormous brand permission to venture into areas other computer companies wouldn't tread.

. . . .

So don't be in a rush to eliminate anything from your list. Continue to be adventuresome and risky, and keep looking at all your potential ideas from as many angles as you can. Yes, you've got a time frame to get the job done. But it's better to have a Big Idea at the start than to rush to market with a "pretty good" or "so-so" idea. Give all ideas the benefit of time and perspective. Be diligent, vigilant, and creative. Take your time. Do it right.

Sifting and Winnowing

A FRIEND OF ours once gave us great advice: "Write drunk," she said, "edit sober." It's time to sober up—but not completely.

If you did a brainstorming session, or if you just gave everyone a period of time to submit ideas, it's now time to size up everything you've got—and sit with it for a while.

As we said before, don't be in a rush to throw out ideas. Simply tossing aside an entire idea because your initial reaction is negative makes no sense. It's a lot more valuable to sift and refine. Examine each idea closely, sifting through the essence of the idea for the elements that can work and discarding the elements that are unworkable. You will often find kernels of good ideas hidden within ideas that aren't feasible on the surface. These can be refined and altered in some way as you work toward your Big Idea. You need to take your time and let things simmer a while.

But at some point you'll know you're done. Or maybe not. Maybe you've got an avalanche of ideas from your team or your company, and you want to make a preliminary cut. Either way, it's time to step back, take a deep breath, and start asking yourself if there's something to work with among all those ideas. Begin by seeing if you've got a slam-dunk winner.

. . . .

CASE IN POINT

Advertising executive George Lois told this story years ago in his autobiography, George, Be Careful. *His agency was working with Aunt Jemima and the company was waffling (sorry, we couldn't resist the pun) about manufacturing maple syrup. The agency's president went out on the street to conduct an impromptu survey, and asked passersby what brand of maple syrup they used with their pancakes. Many of the people he surveyed claimed that they were already using Aunt Jemima syrup. How's that for a slam-dunk winner? It was so logical that Aunt Jemima could be/should be in the maple syrup business that consumers already believed it was in their pantries. It's an example of consumer acceptance before the product was even created.*

. . . .

By the way, putting a slam-dunk idea in front of senior management is an easy way to see whether they're committed to moving forward with the Big Idea you come up with. If they don't buy into the easy idea, they're just humoring you. And if that's the case, the company is likely in trouble for the long term, and you'd be wise to update your resume.

CASE IN POINT

This is more a cautionary tale rather than an example; it also comes under the heading of "coulda/shoulda." Once upon a time, Rolodex owned the business-contact market. If you're under 30, you've probably heard the name, but may not have any idea of who they are or what they did.

Mosey down to the accounting department. Find someone way back in one of those dark, forbidden cubbyholes. You know the office we're referring to: the walls are permeated with 20 years of smoke (even though they stopped smoking in the office years ago) and the gray-haired man or woman hunched over the piles of paper looks positively fossilized. Find that person and ask him or her to show you their Rolodex. If it's not sitting on their desk, they'll open a lower file drawer and pull out this round . . . thing.

The point is that Rolodex could have become Palm Pre. Or iPhone. Or Blackberry. They tried for a while. In the early 1990s, there was a brief period before PDAs when stores sold "digital address books" and Rolodex tried to come out with a branded version via a licensing agreement. But they didn't have the corporate wherewithal to move into the digital marketplace. Our hunch? A very senior management team was no longer hungry. But whatever the reason, they just didn't compete in the PDA sphere—and now they are a quaint, curious business sidebar.

Let's say you're not sure if there's a no-brainer idea in the pile. Or let's say there's an idea or two with the potential to be a massive hit—but will require a huge commitment on the part of the company. The only way to evaluate it is by whatever you wrote down back in Chapter 8 ("Parameters and Process"). If you haven't put together a set of criteria for what a new Big Idea should do, then you haven't got a basis on which to evaluate the ideas.

So, if you haven't done that yet, do it now. Go back and review Chapter 8. Write down what you think the criteria should be for any new idea. Post that list prominently on a wall in the war room. What does the idea need to be to qualify as a Big Idea? What should it do for the business? And most important, will it meet the test of reasonableness?

The Test of Reasonableness

Let's take a minute and talk about the test of reasonableness. Professional to professional.

Let's say you've gotten far enough along in the process that senior management has bought into the idea of a new Big Idea team and is waiting for you to get back to them. Good for you. But we know that the realities of your particular corporate culture will always be in place. Just because you've sold them on the idea of a Big Idea process doesn't mean they're willing to risk much.

We don't know your corporate culture, so we can't answer exactly how that may all play out for you. But you know, realistically, whether you work for a company that would approve an idea like iTunes (a complete leap outside the traditional parameters for a computer company), or would be happy if you came up with a king-size box. ("It's an innovation. We can make more money on each sale. There's no big risk.")

That's what we mean by the test of reasonableness: knowing what your company management is like, does the idea in front of you have a reasonable chance of getting approved? And does it have a reasonable chance of taking off in the marketplace?

A classic story that Steve remembers from childhood was something he believes he read in *Readers Digest* as a 10-year-old. It had to do with a guy approaching the matchbook companies and offering to save them a ton of money—provided they gave him a percentage of the savings for the rest of his life. The companies tried to figure out what that savings could be, and finally gave up and signed the agreement. At that point, the gentleman said, "Remove the striking surface from one side of your matchbox." The two-sided striking surface was ubiquitous, so the manufacturers could no longer see it. It took an outsider to save them money—and make money for himself.

Sounds quaint and apocryphal, but the person who came up with the idea was a hero. And you could be, too. Let's be honest, here: if you and your team come up with a simple, easy-to-implement idea that saves the company millions, you'll be a big winner. As in, "Hey, guys, why don't we have a timer that shuts the building's lights off at 10 PM?" (You probably do, but someone came up with that idea!)

So, start sifting and winnowing the ideas and put them into buckets. Sort them any way you want—from easiest to implement to hardest, from lowest cost of participation to bet-the-ranch. The categories you create will be a function of the parameters you established.

Examine multiple sorts of ideas across multiple criteria. "Last man standing" may be your best and biggest idea. In sifting and winnowing, the Big Ideas need to overcome numerous analytical obstacles for you to elevate them to the viable candidates you will want to recommend and pursue.

What to Do with the BHAG

There's a matter to discuss here—an ethical dilemma that you may encounter. That is, what happens if you and your team come up with the biggest, best, boldest idea imaginable—a BHAG (Big Hairy Audacious Goal)? And maybe it is an idea that could make the company—or whoever did it—multiple millions or billions of dollars?

First, understand that you are legally and ethically required to present the idea to them. Even if the idea is outside the scope of the company. Show them the idea, and give senior management a chance to say yes or no.

Next, what if they say no? Is it something you totally or strongly believe in? Do you want to approach the company and make a deal to own the idea yourself?

Whatever you do, don't try to sneak it away. Be direct. And honest. And work with the company to figure out how to make it a win-win situation.

• •
CASE IN POINT

Carter Bryant, the inventor who developed Bratz dolls, was working at Mattel when he designed the dolls. His new company, MGA Entertainment, marketed the product line and turned it into a billion-dollar phenomenon. Until Mattel sued them. To date, MGA has lost most of the lawsuits and appeals. At best, the matter of who owns the product line and has the rights to it is unclear. It's a huge brand success in turmoil.
• •

Back in the early 1990s, Steve's now-retired partner, Jeff Woll, proposed a BHAG to Ogilvy & Mather (O&M). It was an idea that was a good 15 years ahead of its time. At first, O&M agreed to develop it, and Jeff started working with teams of programmers at MIT's Media Lab. But as costs grew, O&M senior management became disenchanted with the project. And when Sir Martin Sorrel bought the Ogilvy Group, he was more than happy to give Jeff all the rights to the idea, and everything that had been developed on it to date, as Jeff's severance package. Several years later, Jeff sold the idea to IBM and has been happily lowering his golf score in Florida.

So while you owe the company 100 percent of your energy and efforts, you should also keep open the possibility that your once-in-a-lifetime opportunity might be coming your way if your company doesn't have the conviction or commitment to follow your dream. Stay honest. Stay focused. But if the company gives you the opportunity, carpe diem!

STEP FIVE

*Build Momentum
for the Idea*

Determine the Dimensions of the Idea

MANY YEARS ago, Steve was a junior copywriter and learned a life lesson about new products. He worked on a mid-size peanut butter account when the company was introducing a new line of peanut butters: peanut butter and jam, peanut butter and jelly, peanut butter and marshmallow, and peanut butter and crisped rice. Of the four, the crisped rice one sounded least appealing—and Steve never tried the product before developing the ad campaign. Well, of course, the peanut butter and crisped rice turned out to be the biggest seller of the four, and when Steve, out of curiosity, decided to try it, he discovered it was delicious. So much for assumptions. And since then, he's always been sure to be the consumer before he starts marketing any product.

How big an idea do you have? The answer is—you don't really know and there's probably no way (before you bring it to market) that you ever can know. That's the problem we have with most "new idea" or "Big Idea" books. They all tell you to find something that stands out—but they don't tell you how. Not really. Because they're unwilling to admit that there's no way to know if something will catch fire.

No one knows what idea will ever really take off.

Yes, we all hope we know. Yes, we all think the idea we've come up with is the one that will zoom to the top. But the simple fact is that no one knows, no one can predict, no amount of testing, pre-testing, focus grouping, or digital razzle-dazzle will ensure a success. And no one ever said it better than the screenwriter William Goldman, in his book *Adventures in the Screen Trade*: "Nobody knows anything. Not one person in the entire motion picture field knows for a certainty what's going to work. Every time out it's a guess."

He wasn't saying people were stupid. He was saying that despite all the knowledge, brainpower, creative skill, research, and testing that's done, at the end of the day no one knows whether a picture will gross a million dollars or a billion.

Same for you. And if that's bad news, and you feel like we've just ripped you off for the price of this book—well, you're missing the point. Because if you proceed with the knowledge that nobody knows, you have a better chance of succeeding than people who think they know or think they can find out—but haven't gone through the hard work and disciplined process to put all the potential winning pieces in place.

Got it? Okay, now let's get back to work. You've developed some great ideas. You're really excited. You've winnowed them down and now you think you've got a couple of winners. Now's when you have to hunker down to identify every weakness, vulnerability, and possible competitor to each Big Idea. Because if you don't, we guarantee the marketplace will.

SWOT

Start with a SWOT analysis of the idea: Its strengths, weaknesses, opportunities, and threats. Or, as we like to say, SWTO (Sweet-O): strengths, weaknesses, threats, and opportunities. Because even though SWOT makes for a great acronym, "threats" generally follow from "weaknesses" and "opportunities" arise from "threats."

Get your team together and have everyone think of all the strengths your new product or service or process has. List them all on an easel sheet on the wall, where everyone can look at them, add to them, and build on them. Maybe you'll have 2 strengths, maybe 20. (If you've got only two strengths, you're probably in trouble unless those two strengths are "Ends global warming" and "Ends global hunger.")

Once you've got all the strengths listed, break your team into three groups and have each group work on one of the remaining items. So one group will focus on weaknesses, one on threats, and one on opportunities. Tell each group to use the "strengths" list as their reference point, so that for every strength there should be a corresponding weakness, threat, and opportunity.

When they've all done their lists, bring the groups back together and combine all the lists. Ta-Dah! An instant, 30-minute SWOT analysis. Isn't that Sweet-O?

Now, take a look at the threats list. Your goal is to turn every threat into an opportunity. And sometimes you won't have to make any changes! So, if you've written as a threat "The ugliest doll ever designed," that might also be its opportunity: "The Ugliest Doll Ever!"—to wit, the Uglydoll collection from Pretty Ugly, LLC, has been a significant and growing marketplace hit.

What we're talking about here borders on marketing—and we certainly hope a marketing person is part of your Big Idea team. But marketing is an essential element of any Big Idea. In fact, there might be some Big Ideas that are nothing but marketing.

- -

CASE IN POINT

FedEx launched its business as Federal Express, and they took on the whole idea of package delivery in general. Their original ad campaign promise was, "When It Absolutely, Positively Has To Be There Overnight," and they traded on the rising business angst about speed and reliability. At the time there were plenty of delivery services (including the U.S. Postal Service) and no shortage of overnight couriers. But no one had made urgency—expressed as an overnight promise—their business proposition. So for the original launch of Federal Express, their entire business model was mostly a marketing ploy attached to a promise. It built confidence and the Federal Express business.

- -

The Short Version of Your Idea

When you think you've got it all covered, see if you can come up with the simplest, clearest, most concrete expression of the idea. What you're looking for isn't the tag line (although if you come up with that, good for you). What you're looking for is the elevator speech. Or as they say in Hollywood, the pitch line. It's a short, one-sentence (or less) expression that can easily be understood by everyone you're going to be presenting the idea to.

"The largest ocean liner in the world hits an iceberg and sinks on its maiden voyage."

"Premium coffee served fast-food style at every street corner."

"The world's meanest, nastiest, bitchiest line of dolls."

"A new search engine."

Hint: If you can't explain your new idea in that succinct a manner, it's probably not going to launch. Because if you can't even explain it clearly and simply within your own organization, how will you explain it to the world? It should be fairly easy to come up with the concrete expression, since that expression is probably why you thought of the idea in the first place.

Brand Definition

Now, ask yourself whether the new idea will expand or alter the definition of your brand. Are you going from "Apple Computer" to "Apple Inc."? Or from IBM (hardware) to IBM (software)? From McDonald's burgers and fries to McDonald's restaurants? Take a look at every aspect of the new idea and see if it expands the very definition of your brand. If it does, you'll need to factor that into your marketing and product rollout.

You might want to plan on some research to determine whether you've got "brand permission" to move into the broader area. This is tricky, since it involves consumer perception of your brand—and you'll be messing with the mother lode. Apple had consumer permission to move into iTunes. And from there, they had permission to move into iPod, iPhone, and iGotta-Buy-Some-Apple-Stock. We doubt they did any consumer research to "ask permission." This is a confident, innovation-based company. And they are moved by inventions that respond to consumer lifestyle changes.

On the other hand, Coke did do research in the early 1980s, and then made two ill-fated moves: one we already mentioned (they tried to launch a clothing line); the second was that they tinkered with the secret formula to their powerful brand. More on this when we discuss due diligence (Chapter 17). Both turned out to be consumer moves for which Coca-Cola had no consumer permission. So if you're going to be expanding or redefining the brand, you should know that could be an "all-in" bet.

Extendibility

Is your new idea extendable? Can you go from basic Gatorade to a full line of flavored sports drinks? Apparently, yes. And can you then go from flavored sports drinks to enhanced sports drinks? Take a look at your new idea and see where it will lead you three, five, and ten years out. Then ask yourself whether you want to roll out the extensions one at a time or all at once. The answers to those questions will impact timing, marketing, budgeting, and manufacturing.

Where Will the Idea Live?

Are you going to be fighting for shelf space in your local supermarket, or are you going to live in the digital universe? Can you sell your innovation in vending machines? Could you sell it via infomercials and never need a retail location?

List all the places you think your new idea can live—and make a list of pros and cons for each vehicle. If the answer to the question is, "all of the above," that may be exciting news, but you'll need to prioritize the order in which you want to roll out the idea.

. . . .
CASE IN POINT

Everyone thinks of Best Buy as a big-box store. But Best Buy has been very nimble in exploring multiple platforms for distribution. Yes, they have their stores. Yes, they have their Web site. But if you look at the layout of the stores, you'll notice that they're organized like an electronic department store: there are separate zones and departments for each technology. In addition, they've opened some brick-and-mortar wireless stores, which carry every major wireless phone service and every accessory for every type of portable phone.

In mid-2009, Steve stumbled across a Best Buy vending machine at the Memphis airport. It was an elaborate Japanese-style vending machine that had every possible electronic device for the road warrior, from car-phone chargers to iPods to DVDs to noise-canceling headsets. Clearly, someone at Best Buy rethought the definition of "big box" and realized that a very focused "small box" offering could extend both the brand and sales "on the road."
. . . .

Consumers and Markets

Ask yourself: "Who's my audience and what's my market?" If your answer is "everyone," you're going to get into big trouble on your rollout. You can't be all things to all people. And, even if you were, you couldn't possibly afford the marketing budget needed to reach everyone.

Focus. Focus. Focus.

If your idea requires marketing, it's essential that you start to wrap your arms around it before you go to launch. At this point in your process you don't have to come up with a detailed marketing strategy and media allocation, but you do have to have some idea of what it's going to take and what it's going to cost to break through and win in the marketplace. Management will certainly ask the question once you pitch your Big Idea.

Which leads you right into this last question: What are your platforms? Web? Television? Radio? Direct mail? Point of purchase? YouTube? Facebook? Twitter? The platforms you choose for your marketing say a lot about who your company is and how you want the public to perceive you. Going the infomercial route? Advertising in the subways? Viable vehicles, but some companies have self-image problems with certain media. Marketing via YouTube? Facebook? Twitter? Be looking for a highly viral idea and brilliant execution.

16

Research

FOR EVERY novelty product that becomes a big success, there are hundreds (probably thousands) that never see the light of day. Pet Rocks, Chia Pets—who woulda thought? Or novelty toys? Slinky, hula hoop—for each of these products there was an idea. Maybe a Big Idea, maybe not. But it was an idea that caught fire with consumers.

They were launched. They took off. The rest is history. But unless you have very deep pockets and an incredibly trusting management, you're not getting to market without vetting the opportunity for your idea. It's time for research.

But this is tricky stuff. That's because research is best for assessing what is known, not what is unknown or so innovative that consumers may not have a reference point for it. Still, you've got to get some kind of useful research in hand. The design of what you set out to learn is critical.

- -
CASE IN POINT

When an entrepreneur out of Cleveland, Georgia, invented a new line of dolls with an elaborate backstory, he shopped it at every major toy company. Xavier Roberts's Cabbage Patch Kids were chubby rag dolls with unusual faces. His idea was that every one of them was to be different, uniquely named, and adopted by young children. A number of companies were fascinated by the proposition but they didn't know what to make of it. At least one of the companies decided to research the idea as a first step in considering taking on the line. Good idea.

But their research design yielded two important pieces of feedback that derailed their consideration of the line.

- *Girls didn't understand the concept of adoption.*

- *The dolls were not classically beautiful.*

Both were good and true answers. But they were answers to the wrong questions. As the phenomenon of Cabbage Patch Kids showed, young kids certainly understood the idea of personalization and parenthood ("I promise to be a good parent to my Cabbage Patch Kid."). They were swept up by their individual looks and unique and personal names. The departure from classic doll beauty made the dolls vulnerable and accessible to the millions of kids who became parents to Cabbage Patch Kids.
- -

The burden of research for new ideas is on being very creative and complete. Seek to learn how the idea can connect with consumers—not why it won't. Tap into a behavior that may be leverageable, and successful vetting may be your reward.

A strategic planner at the Goodby, Silverstein & Partners advertising agency had an insight about milk that fueled a focus-group design that led to the "Got Milk?" campaign. The idea was that milk is a singular beverage that people find indispensible with certain foods. Focus-group attendees were told not to consume any milk for a week before the research. Well, imagine. On the day of the research, the participants were fired up. They had desperately missed not having milk with their coffee. They had to forgo eating cold breakfast cereal. And the thought of a chocolate chip cookie or a piece of chocolate cake without milk—What, are you kidding me? The insight was real. People want—dare we say need?—their milk with certain and specific foods. The "Got Milk?" campaign drives home this strategic insight in a series of wonderfully dramatic moment-of-truth executions.

The "Got Milk?" research was designed to tap into a consumer behavior that could be translated into motivating messaging. On the other hand, the Cabbage Patch Kids research tapped into conventional wisdom that provided no avenue for alternative thinking, for reception—indeed, for absolute adoration of the dolls.

The other huge caveat about research on a new idea actually embraces some of the dynamics of conventional wisdom. Brand permission suggests that there are places a brand can go and places it can't. So a Big Idea needs to have its roots in current consumer behavior, but extend that reach to places the consumer will be delighted to go.

· ·
CASE IN POINT

Brand Coca-Cola realized they had a problem when they observed in research that young people preferred the sweeter taste of Pepsi to Coke. Through diligent blind taste-testing research, a formulation that became New Coke was tested against Pepsi and performed better than classic Coke. The research was promising, and Coca-Cola brought New Coke to the marketplace. There was only one problem—one huge problem. People don't live in a blind taste-test world. So when consumers drank New Coke, they rejected it because it didn't taste like Coke. In a mad scramble to remedy the marketing fiasco, Coca-Cola relaunched the original-formula Coke as Coca-Cola Classic and let New Coke slowly die a painful death.

· ·

The moral of the story is that research is critical. But it needs to be complete. It needs to simulate the real world. It needs to assess consumer reaction to the big new idea in the context in which consumers will confront and use it. Be mindful. Be creative. Be insightful. But, above all, be "consumer complete" in your vetting of what can make your idea a winner.

17

Due Diligence

SEVERAL YEARS before Steve arrived at NBC, the promotion department had redesigned the company logo and was using a block-letter N in two colors, half in red, half in blue. After winning approval from everyone in the company, and spending a small fortune on stationery, business cards, program promotional artwork, signage, and the thousands of other corporate logo applications, they announced the new logo to the world—only to find it was virtually indistinguishable from Nebraska Public Television's logo. Nebraska Public Television got to fund many of its programs for the next few years from the money NBC paid them to get the rights to the two-color N. Oops!

Somewhere in the process, you've got to bring in the lawyers. There are two solutions. Which you should use is a function of your company's size.

The first approach is to get management buy-in and approval, then get the lawyers involved before going much further in the idea's development. The reasoning? The first instinct of most corporate lawyers is to say no. And if the lawyers say no, there isn't a whole lot you can do about it. Granted, they should know that your development team is blessed by management, but they won't always have the highest incentive to make the idea real.

But if the lawyers are brought in after management has said yes, then generally the lawyers will work that much harder to find ways to make the idea happen. ("We can't do this? Do you really want me to go back to Bill/Sergei/Steve/Jeffrey and tell him you said no?") The problem with that second approach is that you might, indeed, have an idea that, for whatever reason, cannot be done legally. You're going to look very bad having expended all that time and energy (not to mention wasting the CEO's time making your presentation) on an idea that can't be done.

Obviously, calling in the lawyers second makes much more sense if you have no in-house counsel, your company is small, and it's easier to pitch and develop ideas without incurring the outside costs of an attorney. But the approach in big companies is to make one of the attorneys a member of the Big Idea team.

In fact, an ideal strategy is to invite one of your company's lawyers to serve as the executive secretary of the team. Have him take notes. Have him record everything that's said and done. And have him be responsible for checking on possibilities and the feasibilities throughout the process. Of course, this will depend on the level and time available of your legal representative.

The advantage of playing it this way is that, all of a sudden, the attorney has a strong incentive to make the idea happen. He or she is crucial to the team's success and can start doing trademark, patent, logo, design, name, and sales mark searches at every step of the way. Sometimes a key idea can be saved if the attorney has a minimal budget to buy URLs and start the registration process along the way.

A few years ago, Steve and his brother, Paul, started co-hosting a radio call-in talk show about the movies, which they titled "Talking Pictures." As soon as they had the initial idea and the initial sales materials, they bought the domain name and asked their attorney to file a registration—and it's a good thing they did. Between filing the registration and getting approval, a film professor at NYU filed for the same trademark for a popular course he was teaching. The professor did everything he could to wrest the trademark away from them, but because they'd started the process before the professor, the trademark office awarded the name to Steve and Paul.

The attorneys will anticipate ways your idea can be stolen, attacked, and defeated. But equally important, they'll find ways to protect your ideas from everyone—including yourself!

Budgets

BACK IN THE 1980s, Steve went out to Hollywood to try his hand at scriptwriting. He'd written a TV pilot that Osmond Television Productions wanted to develop, and he took the opportunity to give it a shot. When he arrived in L.A., he found a brilliant entertainment lawyer to help him negotiate the deal. After the deal was in place, the attorney gave Steve some advice about "the business" that has served him well ever since.

"At the start of every meeting," the attorney told him, "ask the people around the table how much money you're going to be walking out with right now. Not "down the road" or "if the deal goes." Not "if we sell your script." Not any kind of promises of "back end," "net," or "revenue sharing." Just ask them: 'How much money are you paying me right now?' Believe me," he finished, "That question will save you an enormous amount of time in this town."

As excited as you are, or as excited as you've made management, they're going to want to know about the numbers. So, why did we suggest you have a meeting with management without your full plan in place? You know that's what they want to know. That's how they operate—"Yeah, yeah, thanks for the idea, what's it going to cost us?" That's exactly the point.

You want them to fall in love with the idea, just as you did. The more they love the idea, the easier it's going to be to find the money and find a way. Ideas are pure and they are precious. Passion carries lots of weight. Fall in love first; then, plan the wedding.

Management loves you. They love your idea. But you've still got to do the hard work, which is: what's it all going to cost? Yes, it's time to confront both the time and the money demons. Be creative with your planning and scaling. Just as all ideas are not created equal, all plans aren't, either. Can you launch your idea on a beer budget? Or will it take champagne? Consider both paths to market, or even more options in between.

Scaling and Monetizing—Start Big

Your idea development has been all about thinking big. Your budgeting and planning should also be about thinking big. What does a full-tilt plan look like? What will it cost to achieve everything you envision your go-to-market plan will require? What are all of the dimensions and elements of the big-budget launch? Put every element on a spreadsheet and price it.

The Spreadsheet Is Your Friend

Now, open your thinking to other alternatives. You've identified every possible support element for a plan. It's time you perform any necessary triage. You can pick and choose from all your line items to scale plans that you believe can work, but don't require caviar spending.

You know what the sky looks like. Beyond your champagne and caviar budget, what does a high, best, and low budget exercise reveal? And what are the levels you set for "high," "best," and "low" in exploring this exercise? (Remember, every industry has different conventions. Also remember that whatever budget level you set you're going to require a commensurate return on that investment to meet top-line and bottom-line goals.) What are the give-ups in the scaled-down plans? How are the highest and lowest budgets viable?

No budget is of any use to anyone if you don't believe it will achieve your mission. Keep that in the forefront of your thinking as you scale and monetize. But definitely do not walk into management with one take-it-or-leave-it budget plan. It makes it too easy for them to leave it.

Look for New Money

The fastest way to kill your idea—or have it killed by others— is to ask for the development, distribution, sales, or marketing to come from existing budgets. This will immediately alienate anyone who might have been your ally. Budgets are precious, fought over, and fought for. Suggesting your new Big Idea be paid for out of existing brand budgets is, well, suicidal. People own those budgets and they have responsibilities to meet them.

On the other hand, if you work with other departments you can build allies by asking them how much incremental money they'll need to properly launch the Big Idea. Telling them that you're looking for more money for their department is going to make you their new, instant buddy. In addition, figuring out the burn rate on your plan to keep it as low as possible on a monthly basis—learn as you go—will also win you friends and supporters.

Manage Expectations—Feet to the Fire

Building the budget is a critical first step in creating your plan. This is what will get your idea to market. You've got to manage expectations, and the first of these expectations is your own. What are you looking to achieve? Over what period of time? At what cost? With what return? Heard that before?

Think of the budget as investment, not cost, and build your plan accordingly. For every dollar you plan to spend, what is your expected return on that investment? This will be a critical semantic part of the management sell when you present your full-blown plan. Everyone wants to know: What do I get for shelling out cash?

You need to put your own feet to the fire. Make sure you totally believe that the priced elements that will go into your plan are important, viable, and integrated. Otherwise, ditch them. Every line item will be held up to scrutiny. Make sure you are the first critical screen for this important exercise.

Every Big Idea will have unique budget needs. You need to clearly understand the category in which you're operating, the competitive frame, the barriers and opportunities to find your way into the marketplace. If you've invented a new app, your budget has to include programmers and developers. If your Big

Idea is a new selling benefit of your law firm, you've just got to retrain your partners. Whatever your Big Idea is, once you identify key marketplace variables, make friends with your CFO and go for it!

Management Buy-In

IN THE MID-1960S Gillette launched a new cartridge-type razor system. The "blade" was a piece of wound thin steel inside the cartridge, and you rotated a new part of the wound steel band into place whenever you wanted to "change" blades.

For months, the marketing team and the agencies worked on names for the product: band-o-matic, band-shaver—there were literally hundreds of suggestions. Finally (we were told), the CEO of the company attended a meeting, and after listening to the suggestions, announced his own idea. It was Techmatic, which, of course, became the name of the product, even though it had little or nothing to do with the actual device. Make no mistake whose vote counts most.

Okay, everyone is now very excited. Your team has spent a lot of time and energy to land on a game-changing idea. There is an insulated belief that you've got an idea that is potentially huge. You've created the idea, nurtured it, questioned it, and built it to be where it is today. Now, you've got to sell it to the outside world. Yes, management.

Build Excitement for the Idea

The first thing you need to do is find a way to translate and transfer the excitement you have for your idea to the people who are going to give you the next critical approval to advance that idea. The irony is, the bigger your idea, the more difficult it will likely be to get instant acceptance and approval. After all, it's different. It doesn't look, act, or perform like all the other good ideas that have preceded it. For that reason, you'll need to give it way more care and feeding in the management presentation in order to help the evaluators understand that what you've got is really big, really great.

. . . .

CASE IN POINT

The now very famous case of Post-it Notes is a relevant point of reference here. Imagine being the guy working in R&D, trying to come up with a new adhesive, and landing on a sticky substance that was just sticky enough to adhere to surfaces but not usable as a credible adhesive. It could, however, easily be removed from the surfaces to which it was attached without damaging those surfaces—including paper. In the paradigm of glue, you've created an utter failure. The new way of thinking about this is that you've created an entirely new paradigm: customized stickiness. And the rest is history.

But without management vision, Post-it Notes never would have been born. Out-of-the-box thinking imagined a new world of removable sticky notes for a wide range of applications. If conventional thinking had ruled, the transience of stickiness would have been the death knell of this product that became a powerful new brand.

· ·

The mindset that enabled Post-it Notes is not the norm for management. Management is usually content to be in its comfort zone, guiding the ship on a set course. They keep the operation focused. Everyone is to stay on task and on timetable. The "off course" idea is usually not in the management wheelhouse. So even though you've come this far, and you've had your Big Idea Team greenlighted, don't assume for a minute that selling your idea is going to be smooth sailing. After all, you're going to be looking for a serious financial commitment in order to go forward. More likely than not, unless you've got some very clever sell-in, your idea will be a nonstarter.

The good news is that, if you've done your job well, your entire process and team commitment to date has put management in a different frame of mind. They're expecting something big and different from you.

The Pre-Sell

You're going to present your idea to management. But, to whom? To how many people? At what levels? In how many meetings? Where? When? These are all critical questions to answer before you build your presentation and meeting. But as you do that, you want to carefully consider and manage the dynamics of pre-sell. It's time to engage support for the idea. Yes, we know, we've asked those questions before. But you're at a different stage now—and you've got be thinking about internal sell all over again.

How you do that will be a function of your company's business category, size, and management style. For highly siloed or politicized organizations, some organizations, it might be time to do something that would have been verboten during the precious process of idea development: leak the good stuff. That is, create a plan to share your excitement with selected management players. Make them feel that they know something no one else does. Carefully lay the groundwork for the idea and the upcoming presentation without giving it all away. Get them pumped.

For other companies, especially those that are entrepreneurial and thrive on new ideas, you might want to leak some of the strategic thinking. Plant a seed that could germinate as the solution to a consumer problem—but don't uncover your brilliant solution. ("Hey, wouldn't it be great if there were a phone application that lets you know where the caller was actually, physically located?") Getting people to think about the problem certainly will set the stage for your (brilliant) solution and build or pre-sell receptivity to your idea.

However, with other companies, especially highly structured process-oriented companies, leakage in any form might be unacceptable. For them, it might all be about the show-and-tell at the actual presentation. Still others might want the presentation deck to be about need, size of market, and opportunity. It could all be a numbers game; for them, it's going to be about the due diligence and research as much as it will be about the idea itself.

Use your judgment, know your corporate culture, and figure out the best way forward—it's a delicate stage of the process.

Sign On and Sign Off

Don't treat this phase of your process lightly. Every stage of idea development is important. Building belief is critical, too. To date, management has signed on to your process and your team. Getting sign-off for the idea means that you will next be looking for major commitments of budget—that's both big bucks and significant staff time allotted to date.

But management sign-off here is not about asking for a budget or looking for sign-off on your implementation plan. That will come later. What makes this step critical is that it's a momentum-builder. It puts management in the frame of mind to support you: to put the money where, to date, only their mouths have been.

Remember, you've lived with this idea for weeks and months. You're totally committed to it and you're unabashedly enthusiastic about it. But it's going to be new to management, so you've got to recapture—for them—your initial enthusiasm, your doubts, your objections overcome, your beliefs and realizations—all the emotional, tangible, and rational elements that led you to recommend this one particular Big Idea.

Building the Presentation

Once again, you'll need a great presentation—a simple, clear, compelling presentation. You're selling one thing and one thing only—your idea. But the key is to romance it. Remember the key aspects of selling presentations: tell them what they're going to see, tell them why they're going to like it, give them rationale for why the idea is so great, present the idea, tell them why it's so great, remind them about why they love it so much. And, then, and only then, ask for their comments (about how much they love the idea). This is an artful process. It needs to be stealthy, not obvious that you are selling your heart out.

Making the Presentation

You've pre-selected your management audience. Perhaps you've planted pre-sell believers in the management crowd. You've determined your venue, time, and attendees (both from your team and the management approvers). Now, you determine the length of the presentation, those who will present, and what the endgame looks like. What do you want from this group? Agreement to go to plan? Permission to take the idea to the next management level? Empower the people in the room. Make them feel as important as your idea is.

From Here to Eternity

Place clear parameters around the sign-off. Make it obvious that this is not a final meeting. There will be other steps and other checks and balances before the idea commands a huge expenditure of time and money. Provide a road map for what comes next.

You build a plan. The plan has clear parameters of what you expect to do, and what you intend to achieve. The plan outlines the budgets, timing, key milestones, and metrics. (The plan will be explained in greater detail in Chapter 20, "What Should the Plan Look Like?") Key here is to provide management with the freedom to believe that you're not looking for a blank check—that there will be major checkpoints along the way as you take your idea from here to maternity to eternity.

So go ahead—make that sale! After all, your company's future is riding on it.

STEP SIX

Develop the Plan

What Should the Plan Look Like?

A FEW YEARS ago, Paul was putting an addition on a modest lake cabin. It was a small project and the architect was focused on a much bigger design for a major new estate. Though responsive to Paul, he advanced the project only when Paul pressed for meetings. At other times, the drawings were delegated to his junior draftsmen.

When the drawings were completed, and all the town and lake association approvals were in hand, construction got under way. Fortunately, Paul checked in on the builder on a regular basis. On one visit, the builder expressed frustration that the new master-bedroom closets didn't connect to the ceiling. The architect had left out of the plans all the elevations on what was to be a room with a cathedral ceiling. Paul called the architect, who immediately realized the grave error of his omission. Within 24 hours, three new interior plan options were forwarded to Paul. One worked great. Thank goodness plan implementation hadn't gone beyond rough carpentry. The aggravation, expense, and time lost for an incomplete plan could have been a disaster.

So what do you need to include in your plan? The simple answer is, everything you need to make the sale. The more complete and complicated answer is, everything you'll need to get the resources, support, and team to give the idea its best shot at getting to and succeeding in the marketplace.

For a wide array of marketing pointers, we refer you to our book *The Little Blue Book of Marketing: Build a Killer Plan in a Day* (Portfolio, 2010). This will give you a head start on all the marketing elements you need to consider and include to put your Big Idea on plan. Consider the following checklist but adopt and adapt at will to empower your best sale:

- Vision

- Mission

- Competitive frame

- SWOT

- Positioning

- Budget and rationale

- Paths to market

- Media selection (toolkit)

- Strategic partners

- Action steps and milestones

- Integrated marketing flowchart (with budget breaks)

- Dream team

- Timing/next steps

- Implementation

- Research and measurement

Consistent with all the marketing elements that will populate your plan, you're going to need a good set of financials. What spending will you require to support your idea? For what? And over what period of time? You're also going to need detailed market implementation planning, timing, and metrics. What do you intend to do over what period of time, and to what anticipated positive effect? How do you want your success to be measured? Don't overpromise. Don't underpromise. Management likes success, but never likes an unplanned-for surprise.

• •
CASE IN POINT
Google is nothing short of a phenomenon. Back in the day, who knew that search was going to be such a powerful people and business model? Not Microsoft, AOL, or Yahoo!. But with incredible utility as the driver of finding all sorts of information on the Web with ease, Google became the killer app of a new online behavior. And advertisers flocked to the medium in droves. Voilà! A very profitable business.

YouTube took the world by storm as well. As the repository for videos of all kinds, YouTube was where people posted their random content. Google bought the business. But as of this writing, YouTube has yet to become profitable. Hugely popular, yes. Profitable, no. Is Google sorry they own YouTube? Certainly not. But what were the planning components that went into the YouTube acquisition? Certainly it was to corner the market with the leading player in videos. But if management had built a plan calling for huge YouTube profitability out of the box, there would be great disappointment—and, likely worse—in Mountaindale.

Just ask eBay how they feel about the Skype acquisition today.

• •

Even the big boys buy with emotion. Building a plan to set business expectations is as critical as building a plan to set a business in motion.

21

Sell the Plan

THIS IS THE third time we've talked about selling. That's because selling happens at each key stage of your process. First, you sold the idea of seeking a Big Idea. Then, you sold the Big Idea. Now, you've got to sell the plan to enable the Big Idea. Yes, every great Big Idea needs to be sold and resold.

Back to Paul's lake house. Paul had the idea to put a trail around one of the lakes that his homeowners' association owns. He brought the idea to the conservation committee, who suggested the idea be presented to the board of directors. The board of directors approved the low-impact taping of a trail, to be brought back to them for final approval. The marked trail was then represented to the board with a map to show ingress and egress and trail geography. The board then approved the grooming and permanent marking of the trail. All this for a low-impact foot trail. There were at least three or four selling presentations to get the plan approved and the trail execution put into action. Imagine the due diligence you need to go through in selling a multimillion-dollar idea!

In selling your plan, it's critical to protect your idea from naysayers. Anticipate every obstacle. It was cheap for management to buy your Big Idea process, and even your Big Idea itself. The cost in terms of time and money was nominal. The stakes are much greater now. Just because people like your idea, that doesn't mean they'll put their money where their mouth is. You've got to assume that you're going to be rejected, so plan your plan to be profoundly victorious.

Write your plan to disarm the negative and sell the positive. Make it as inviting and creative as the idea itself. Keep a tight cover on the plan for the idea, though. Buzz can be the kiss of death. You don't want lots of people talking about what you're going to do before you make your case. This is delicate stuff.

The selling presentation has got to restate the idea—clearly, completely, and compellingly. Never take for granted that everyone remembers your great idea. Make the idea sound as fresh and powerful as the day you conceived it. Share your positive research on the idea. Affirm the competitive insulation you've built into the idea. Corroborate the legal protection for the idea. Cover all bases, and make management confident that your winner is a home run—indeed, a winner from every imaginable angle.

Provide an action timetable. What are you planning to do next and over what time period? Provide a picture of success. How will you measure results? What is your test plan going to be? What kind of return over what period of time are you expecting? What other metrics will you build into the plan in terms of research or other competitive or marketplace measures that will inspire confidence in and continuation of the pursuit of the Big Idea?

· ·

CASE IN POINT

Star Wars *was one of the biggest movie phenomena of all time. Among other things, it spawned a huge idea from Kenner Toys— the creation of action figures. These 3¾-inch plastic characters revolutionized the boys' toys marketplace.*

Over at Hasbro, the first ever doll for boys—G.I. Joe—had been out of the marketplace for some time, owing to the high cost of plastic and the resulting high price points for a collectible 11-inch male mannequin. Paul's future partners—Tom Griffin, Joe Bacal, and Steve Schwartz, the latter, head of marketing at Hasbro—saw a big opportunity to bring G.I. Joe back for a new generation of boys. The idea was to steal a chapter from Kenner's new product playbook and bring G.I. Joe back as a new scaled-down product line of action figures, vehicles, and accessories with attractive price points. Seemed like a winning idea.

When presented to Hasbro's CEO, Stephen Hassenfeld, he was intrigued, but he ultimately turned the plan down. The thinking was solid, but the plan didn't go far enough. After all, a new generation of kids had seen Star Wars *movies and knew the characters and the plot lines. What did kids of the day know about G.I. Joe? Nothing. So Griffin Bacal went back to the drawing board.*

The resulting plan that came back to Hassenfeld included a plan to create a series of Marvel comics to tell the G.I. Joe story.

New advertising would sell the comics and advance the story. Product would be rolled out consistent with the unfolding of the story, and there would be increasing price points throughout the year leading up to Christmas. And the pièce de résistance, Griffin Bacal's sister production company, Sunbow, would steal a chapter out of Roots, *the mini series, and create a multiple-night TV mini series to seed the story of G.I. Joe. The plan was much richer than the previous one; it was loaded with market-breaking ideas and it was resoundingly approved by Hasbro's CEO. The rest, as they say, is history. Go Joe!*

• •

So, yes, this is the third time we've had a chapter on selling. That's because selling is that important. And one sale will lead to another. The lessons are the same: keep it fresh, keep it exciting, keep it interesting—and keep up everyone's enthusiasm every step of the way for the perils and prospects of stepping out into the void!

22

Who Ya Gonna Call?

AS OUR PUBLISHERS work with us on our books, we always develop a parallel marketing schedule. Working back from the actual date of publication, we decide where we're going to reach our target audience and what we're going to need to reach them. Ads? Prepublication galleys? Bound books? Video? Blogs? Broadcast e-mail? Reviewers? We look at all the "contact points" between us and our potential readers, and we ask what our deliverables will be and by what date. Working off that schedule, we determine who we're going to need to get involved and on what level. Will we need our Web site designer? How much time does her team at Chewy Media need? Are we shooting video? What's Tallboy Films' production schedule? Press? PR? E-mail and mailing lists? Step by step, we outline all the possible players and then we arrange a marketing plan in a day to bring them all together in one key launch session, when the entire program gets built.

Take a lesson from *Ferris Bueller's Day Off*: If you're going to do it, do it right. And doing it right might involve a lot more players than you initially imagined.

You're still a ways from the finish line, but you're beginning to see the light at the end of the tunnel. Just make sure it's not a freight train coming the other way. From this point on, you need the most organized, buttoned-up members of the team to step forward and start doing their parts to move the plan ahead. This is your dream team.

Will you need a prototype? Will you need patents? Will you need a new Web site? A new URL? Manufacturers? Partners? Vendors? New equipment? Since we don't know what your breakthrough idea is, we can't give you an automatic checklist. You've figured a lot of that out in writing and selling in your plan. But, for the really granular elements of making it all happen, that's the focus of your next meeting and planning session.

· ·

CASE IN POINT

Procter & Gamble (P&G) are masters of marketing—and they're constantly searching for ways to reach that launch point as economically and effectively as possible. Many years ago, they used to depend on test markets. Which meant they had to develop the prototypes, manufacture significant quantities of the product, build a marketing plan, shoot their commercials

*and print ads, run their media tests, and measure the results. An
expensive and time-consuming process.*

*These days, P&G uses the Web—especially for products
they're targeting to the under-30 set. We keep visiting the Swash
site because it keeps evolving its message, test videos, honing
the message and homing in on their customers' "hot buttons."
There is wisdom in their using the Web for research as well as
running inexpensive, rough-test TV spots, to find the most effective message at a fraction of the price they used to spend for test
market implementation. Bravo!*

As you get a handle on the scale and scope of your needs,
start drawing up the names of individuals and companies on
your action team.

First, you're going to need your lawyers. You're going to
want scorched-earth, bomb-proof competitive insulation. Are
you confident you've got a product, service, or process no one
can duplicate in the next 12 months, even if they have the
blueprints?

Then, maybe you want to deliberately leak some news to the
blogosphere to test peoples' reactions to the idea. If there's a
loud "I gotta have that!" chorus, you might want to rush ahead.
If it falls on deaf ears, you might need to do some research and
probe more to find out why no one's as excited as you are.

CASE IN POINT

*Fragrance-industry manufacturers are masters at saving devel-
opment dollars. At Fabergé, they used to challenge their agency
to come up with a name and concept for a new fragrance. When*

they had five or ten ideas, they would bring focus groups together and ask women which of the fragrance ideas they were most interested in. (At no time did they reveal that they hadn't actually made any of these fragrances.) If no clear winner emerged, the agency went back to concept development. If there was an apparent winner, Fabergé would then take that concept to the fragrance designers, and they would challenge the designers to "create a fragrance that you think smells like this concept."

Again, once they had a half dozen or more sample fragrances they would go into another round of focus-group testing, asking women, "Which of these fragrances do you think matches this concept?" When they had a winner, they went to market! Note— they asked both the agency and the fragrance designers to work for a minimal fee (with the promise of the money they would earn should there be a winning concept). For Fabergé, the cost of R&D was mostly the cost of running the focus groups. Or, as the agency often called them, "the fuckus groups."

. . . .

While one extreme of product development involves all kinds of people and groups to help get the idea off the ground, at the other extreme is total disclosure paranoia. This can be as complicated as making everyone you want involved come to your office, sign individual (not just group) non-disclosure agreements (NDAs), and showing them the concept and not allowing anyone to leave your building with any printouts, samples—nothing! Some companies even bury tracking codes into their digital documents so that, in case there is a leak, the company can track it back to the vendor. We know one company that uses "fake tracking codes." They don't know how to insert hidden code into their documents, so they simply tell their vendors that all the documents have tracking codes and depend on the threat of detection to be the ultimate deterrent.

You have to decide. The greater the secrecy, the slower, more cumbersome, and more expensive the process will become. For example, you might not be able to multiple-bid a job because you don't want the losing bidders to know about the product. You might have to push your timelines if your vendors can work only at your offices and must leave all materials behind when they leave the building.

Part of what will dictate your attitude is the nature of the product itself. Are you building the Aurora? (That's the high-speed spy plane the Air Force has built and flies out of Area 51 to replace the SR-71 Blackbird. Oops. Now that the Air Force knows we know, if something mysterious happens to either one of us, you'll know who did it.) Are you manufacturing the first device of its kind? Are you planning to offer a recyclable container for your product? The level of secrecy has to be driven by two key factors: the impact you expect the idea to have on the marketplace and the amount of lead time you're going to need to bring it to the marketplace. Use your judgment.

Once you've got the list of potential or necessary players, make sure you've got all your legal i's dotted and t's crossed. Then start by organizing your IP (inside players) team.

The IP Team

Borrow a page from the military. As the plan begins to unfold, brief the troops in a top-down manner. You might have had someone from manufacturing as part of your development team, but now that R&D person knows that his boss has to be briefed and other members of the manufacturing team have to become part of the process. *Treat those team members with awe and respect!*

This inside team is going to be the most important part in the execution of the process. Maybe some of them are jealous or resentful that they weren't part of the original team. Maybe they don't want the added responsibility on their plates. You can never know what individual motivations are at work—but you can certainly motivate them, get them jazzed and excited about the idea.

Sell Them Like You Sold Management

Bring this IP team together (all at one time) with all the team members of your brain trust. Make it exciting and celebratory. Tell them that they're the first in the company outside of the board/CEO to know about the idea. Impress upon them the importance of the idea for their careers and the future of the company. Reveal the idea with as much enthusiasm, excitement, and energy as you can muster. Then give them some room to absorb the information.

Answer their questions. Address their concerns (and there will be some concerns; but if you can't overcome the objections/concerns of your internal team, how do you expect to sell the rest of the world?). Let them make a contribution to the overall process. Then show them the developmental timeline and begin to assign schedules and roles to these key players.

In addition to your Big Idea team players who move on with you to the implementation phase, these people are your first-line teammates. They're the ones who will guard the secrets and keep the idea moving. Making them feel needed and appreciated is a key part of building your winning action team. So decide how you're going to work with them, who they're going to be, and start bringing them on board!

STEP SEVEN

The Launch

Let's Do Launch

AS YOU LOOK to bring the idea to market, it might be time to add some additional players. Who you add will be dictated by the type of idea you have and your plan to make it a success. Let's look at what you've got to explore and develop.

Distribution

How are you gonna get the product to the point of sale? And what *is* the point of sale? Retail stores? Wholesalers? Online? One thing is clear today. The price of entry has never been lower. If you're looking to launch on a shoestring, consider a controlled launch online. For sure, you've got to get your distributors involved in the process—and don't forget the lead time they're going to need to ramp up the distribution. But, if you're the distributor, you're in the driver's seat for timing, execution, fulfillment, and cost.

Communication

Who needs to know about this? (Don't forget your B2B partners.) Consumers? Reviewers? A narrow audience segment? Early adapters? Buzz agents? All of these questions are part of the larger advertising/marketing/PR question: Do you have a reliable team to market, advertise, and spread the word about your product or service?

From 1991 to 2001, the chairman of Discovery Communications, Inc. (DCI), John Hendricks, would acquire or launch a new network (or two) almost every year. First, it was TLC. Then Travel Channel. Then Animal Planet. Then discovery.com. Then the Discovery digital networks (Science, etc.). The assumption was always that the company had an award-winning in-house design group that had the knowledge and experience to successfully launch a new network. But knowledge isn't the same thing as manpower.

Under the doctrine of lean marketing, DCI had the people to do the job—and not much more. And every new network launch or acquisition put an added strain on the design department. It was a case of "Just because you have the bodies, that doesn't mean you have the resources."

But in one aspect your job, or the job of your marketing team, should be fairly easy: you arrived at the Big Idea because you thought it was, in fact, a Big Idea. If it truly is a Big Idea, then who you want to reach should be built into the very concept. ("Hey, how about we offer digital music players that customers can use to download songs off the Web, load onto these players, and carry around with them?" Well, you're not going to launch that product aiming at retirees, are you?)

The key decision you've got to make is whether you're going to launch the product in test, launch it as a rollout, or do a national launch. Again, it's something that will be determined by your budget, your resources, and how big the idea is.

. . . .

CASE IN POINT

FedEx is one of the few companies we know that introduced their service (overnight delivery) as a test, rollout, and national launch all at the same time. They knew there was nothing particularly revolutionary about their service (package delivery), but in order to preempt competitors, they had to sell customers on the urgent need for (then) Federal Express, and promise its reliability ("When It Absolutely, Positively Has To Be There Overnight"). So they started advertising nationally—which was fine, except that they weren't available nationally.

If you called up Federal Express from Chicago and asked them to make a delivery to, say, Miami, they would tell you that service wasn't yet available either in (a) Chicago (for pickup) or (b) Miami (for delivery), but it would be, soon. Those calls served as a guide, telling the company where the demand was. As soon as demand reached a threshold for pickup or delivery to a particular city, Federal Express would add that city to their service routes. That way, they expanded their global network by letting the demand for the service shape their shipping grid.

. . . .

If you know your audience, manufacturing costs, price points, and distribution methods, you've already got a good handle on what you need to do.

Maybe it's as simple as sending someone out to try a new selling message. If you've decided to offer a new type of service at your two-person law firm, it should be easy enough to call a few existing clients, tell them about the new service, and gauge their reaction. (Call that "qualitative research.") On the other hand, you might not necessarily want to keep your existing clients—or they might not be interested in the new product or service.

In 2004, our media consultant, Gene DeWitt, said something to us that changed our entire business. Prior to that time we were a creative resource group: we would develop ad campaigns, new product launches, and special promotions for clients whose existing advertising agencies didn't know what to do. It was a good business, but the margins were getting slimmer. Around that time also, Gene said to us, "Well, you know, in five years every company's going to have to have their own network." What he meant by that wasn't a traditional television or cable network (although if you're a Walt Disney or Hallmark or Oprah, maybe that's exactly what you do). What he meant was that every company was going to have to have a 24-hour-a-day, 7-days-a-week digital relationship with its customers. We discussed it and realized he was right—and decided to reshape our company as a digital-content development group rather than a creative resource group.

The result was a change in partners, personnel, and structure. When we told our existing clients, some of them said, "Thanks, we'll be in touch" while others stayed with us. Today, the business is healthier and growing—because the new product/service offering matched the marketplace, not just the needs of our existing clients.

On a macro level, you can look at Big Blue. IBM no longer manufactures personal computers. As they saw PCs becoming commoditized products, they realized the profit margins would become too thin to sustain a viable business. With the acquisition of Lotus, IBM had beefed up their software offerings—so they sold their PC business to Chinese manufacturer Lenovo.

Use your common sense and start calling on all your resources. Pull out those nondisclosure agreements and begin to ramp up the launch team. Then start building the launch model that makes the most sense for your business.

Implement a
Readable Test

EARLY IN HIS advertising career, Paul was the assistant account
executive on P&G's Charmin bathroom tissue. It was not yet a
national brand, but it was the leading brand in virtually all markets
where P&G sold it. Charmin had conquered most of the United
States and was putting the finishing touches on its West Coast
expansion. Market testing was slow, methodical, and vitally important. A test market could easily endure a year or more before rollout was committed. The best packaged-goods marketers
understood this and were very disciplined in their test marketing.
Eventually, Charmin completed its national rollout and became
the powerhouse brand in the bathroom tissue marketplace.

The marketing world moves at a faster pace today. Marketers no longer have the luxury—or budgets—to evaluate products in conventional market testing that was commonplace 25 years ago. Competition is tougher and quicker to react. The trade is more demanding and more impatient to see results. And Big Ideas are more easily and readily knocked off or preempted.

So, protecting a Big Idea is more difficult to accomplish than ever before. But *implementing* a Big Idea has never been easier. Consider several of the huge ideas in the digital and social networking arena. Google, YouTube, Facebook, and Twitter were all viral launches that captured the imagination and massive audiences, seemingly overnight. Access to users over the Internet mitigated expensive TV media campaigns to build awareness, interest, and purchase. Person-to-person communication, both online and in person, drove these brands to become household names. So, too, can other Big Ideas become big market performers.

• •

CASE IN POINT

Procter & Gamble (P&G) was interested in extending its market research muscle to an elusive target audience–teens. At the time, P&G had only about four brands that were targeting this market. So, they both invented a method and invited noncompetitors to be clients of their new model. They called the brand Tremor and today they serve 23 P&G brands and eight non-P&G brands.

The idea was simple. The execution was elegant. They seed nontraditional creative ideas to "connectors"–that very elusive 10 percent of the population who are not only early adopters but are also viral marketers. These are the people who readily try new things—they are the "first on the block." But they also talk about their experiences, share their satisfactions, and attract a wide network of contemporaries to join in the brand.

P&G found that all they needed was 1 percent of the population to make the model work. The key was the proprietary research method that would uncover true connectors and recruit them to be viral marketers. What an elegant business model for learning on the cheap and extending marketing muscle for brands seeking to authentically reach young consumers.

• •

Pick your means and methodology. Qualitative or quantitative research (or both). Old-fashioned one-on-one interviews or high-volume Internet research. There are—literally—hundreds of ways you can get a handle on your audience and their reaction to your Big Idea.

Many years ago, we knew an advertising agency copywriter named Charlie Ryant, who had a sign over his desk, "Guts Is Cheaper Than Research." It was good for a laugh back then—but it's definitely become a lie. Research is cheaper than ever—and the cost of a gut hunch can be enormous.

Today, you can and should get your learning by firing on a lot of cylinders—online hits, visits, research and time spent, in market and trade response, viral, and more. The key here is that, in the digital age, there is more access both to audiences and to learning than ever before. And the cost of this access is lower than ever before, too. So for your Big Idea, you'll want to develop a careful plan to assess how big your idea is and *how big it can be.*

How will you launch? Where will you launch? What marketing and media support will you dedicate to the idea? What different plan alternative might you test? Think direct marketing. You can test different executions, adjust, and test improved efforts.

Read response as you go. Set benchmarks for what you consider success. Make sure you give your efforts a chance to take hold. What are your parameters? What are your milestones? A research plan is critical to enable you to optimize your learning, as well as giving you a greater chance for success. Look for as many learning opportunities as possible. You've come a long way to get that Big Idea into the marketplace. Make sure you give it every best shot to fire away.

A few years back, we were involved in a dot-com startup. Its stated mission was to deliver financial advice for young adults 18 to 34 years old. That's an age range during which a huge number of financial decisions have to be made, and the target audience has the least amount of information. While it was easy for us to make an arbitrary list of needs: student loans, credit cards, first car, first apartment, first house—we really didn't know what the target audience was hungry to understand. For $20,000, we hired MarketTools—an online research company—to give us an in-depth answer to survey questions targeting that audience. The result was a clear, focused analysis of responses to our questions and a practical guide for launching the Web site.

Whatever you decide to do—even if you're a mom-and-pop and your research is about polling friends and family—go out and get some kind feedback before you commit the time and money to making your new dream come true.

25

Read, Roll, or Kill

CHARMKINS WAS a clever collectible idea from Hasbro that fashioned little characters into wearable jewelry. The line was featured in the center of the Hasbro showroom at Toy Fair (the annual primary trade show for the industry) as the big new idea in girls' toys for the year. On a table off in a corner in the same room was another clever idea from Hasbro. The company hoped that small, pastel-colored pony dolls would be received well by the trade—but they didn't put any major emphasis on the product line. The big issue for the year was to be Charmkins. The trade supported both lines, and Charmkins was a modest success. But My Little Pony went on to become an absolute phenomenon.

Not all Big Ideas are created equal. Duh. And the best thinking, rationale, and research can never fully predict how consumers will respond to a product once it hits the marketplace. The key is to read the idea at every level—from concept development through concept research, product development, consumer testing, trade reception, marketing and advertising research, packaging, trade support, retail presence, customer takeaway, and consumer repeat. You get the idea. Measurement matters.

Too often, time and money are dedicated to idea development, but not to idea assessment. It's a mistake. The extra attention, time, and money to develop and field good measurement tools are critical to giving your idea its best shot of becoming a winner. After all, if you don't assess strengths and weaknesses at every step, you can't identify what's working and what isn't. A marketplace launch without meticulous planning and measurement built in will only ensure success, failure, or something in between—without understanding any of the underlying reasons why.

P&G's persistence with Pampers and Pringles was enabled because every step of their failed launches was accompanied by meaningful learning that informed and helped retool the next effort. You can't improve what you don't know. You can't manage what you don't measure.

Measurement Matters

Every business needs to measure success. And every smart business has measures it values to read its marketplace. Big, juicy new ideas are even more critical to measure. And they're even more elusive. The bigger and more uncommon the idea, the more difficult it is to put in place a measurement system of criteria to read success. After all, if the idea has little or no precedent, how can you determine its success? What are the benchmarks against which you'll assess performance?

All of this involves the creative act of research invention. Consumer testing is critical not just to understand customer reception to the new idea but also to project how this new idea will be adopted (and can be adapted) to their lifestyle. Research must be designed in a way that enables responses that might be a complete surprise. Don't "lead the witnesses" when it comes to research. This is a moment when you've got to suspend disbelief and work very, very carefully with a good research methodology. Get the questions right before you start looking for answers.

Measuring customer response to more than one version of the idea can help determine how to proceed. This puts a real premium on good communication of the idea. Virtually as important as the idea itself, communication of the idea in clear, relevant, and compelling ways will drive customer understanding, which leads to customer interest and ultimately to customer takeaway.

. . . .
CASE IN POINT

My Little Pony was a concept born out of a single product offering from Hasbro called My Pretty Pony. My Pretty Pony was a large, hard plastic doll in pony form, with a mane that could be combed. Hasbro's girls' toy group and R&D had the idea that a smaller collectible version of Pretty Pony might be of interest to young girls. Someone had the out-of-the-box idea to consider making the line a series of fantasy ponies in fanciful colors—purple, pink, blue, and so on.

So, two alternative lines of the prospective My Little Pony were tested with young girls. Turns out, the girls were not at all "married to" reality. They loved the fanciful ponies and Pony took off once it hit the toy shelves. And that's the line that came to market (and is with us today, decades later). Charmkins, on the other hand, was quietly discontinued a year later.

. . . .

Inferences and Implications

Drawing inferences and implications is important in product development, and it's a critical activity in assessment, as well. In developing your new idea, you've paid close attention to consumer behavior. It's a game starter. Do you strongly believe that your idea will fulfill a meaningful consumer need or desire? Does your product or service fill a space in the marketplace?

My Little Pony traded on the idea that girls love horses. But built into the concept was the evergreen play pattern that girls love dolls. The product insight was that Pony offered doll and story play in an alternative form. It was unique. Yes, there were realistic collectible horses for girls. But they were all about trophy-case display, rather than hands-on play.

Tuning and Fine-Tuning

Just as a musical instrument needs to be tuned to achieve optimal sound and performance, your product or service needs meticulous tuning and fine-tuning. Success is in the details.

You need to think carefully about the audience for your product or service. Who will want this? Who will use it? Who will love it? Who will talk it up? You need to figure out where and how you'll distribute the product. Is it a mass product? Is it niche? You need to determine the length and breadth of the product line. Will you launch numerous SKUs? What are the price points? What will the year-two and year-three lines look like? There are many examples of marketing ideas that got off to a quick start, and died just as quick a death. Trial is easy. Staying power and brand loyalty are much tougher.

Time to Read

The time to read performance is at every level. Once you commit to the marketplace, you will want to measure customer response quickly and reliably. Set up internal or external methods to read your business. Have up-front goals against which you can assess your progress in sales and over time. Build in go/no-go criteria that will take emotion out of the product expansion equation.

Go or No Go

Go or no go—to launch, to give up, or to give it another go—is always a tough decision. You become passionate about your idea. Your energy and attitude are about going forward. You've dedicated a lot of time and energy to your idea. Your team is committed to what you've achieved. You think you're on to something great. But sometimes the best decision is the no-go decision. Going to market is an expensive proposition. A failure pursued can incur huge losses. An early cancellation or regrouping can be a very inspired decision.

. . . .
CASE IN POINT

Built into the Hasbro Toys R&D process is a steady stream of line reviews. In addition to brand line reviews, there are at least four management line reviews each year. These reviews can last up to three days. That's how long the line is—boys' toys, girls' toys, preschool toys, not to mention the games business. This process is an expensive commitment of time and talent for the company, but it's been an inspired mechanism to get the best minds in the business thinking about new ideas in current and new product lines.

Two dynamics of the process have been especially important in terms of assessing the passion for ideas. The first is the inclusion of the advertising agencies at all line reviews. As a final question in assessing every product line, the agency is asked its point of view. The purpose is to determine—beyond the passion for product—if the agency believes they can communicate the benefit of the product powerfully in 30-second TV commercials. Many products die a quick death if the agency suggests communication would be problematic.

The other tough question posed in line reviews—especially for new product lines—is what would year-two and year-three lines will look like. This fosters a thought process and discipline within R&D that forces the inventors to put their products where their passions are. Does the line have staying power? Will there be exciting product to build the line into more than a one-hit or one-year wonder? It makes for stronger, richer product lines. But it also becomes the Waterloo for lines that are more flash than substance.

. . . .

Again, sometimes an early kill is an inspired move. Directing the idea team to pull the plug on an idea that lacks promise is cost-effective. Challenging the idea team to address the problems and come back with a stronger platform for the idea is smart business.

Reasons to Kill

Sometimes the marketplace tells you in a hurry that your idea just won't launch. But sometimes you can't know for sure why something didn't catch fire. Learn the lessons we've told you about Pampers, Pringles, and other P&G products—always ask yourself two key questions throughout the research and testing phase:

1. Are we asking the right questions? As we mentioned, research can't answer questions about something that doesn't exist. Yes, you can get some indication of how people feel. But if you don't ask the right questions, you're not going to get answers that are of any real use to you. So be sure you're asking the right questions as you go.

2. Is it the product or the positioning? Why isn't (or is) the product launching? Is it the product—or the way it's being marketed? One of the most important things you've got to decide in advance with your marketing group and outside marketing partners is how they plan to answer a simple question: "How will we know if this works?" Make everyone in the process accountable for concrete answers to that question.

Sometimes the idea will survive and thrive. Sometimes the best wisdom is to back away from the idea. Read, roll, reread, kill, or launch should be the mantra of every new product team. Part of the ongoing decision process is how deep your conviction is that the idea is right. Another key criterion has to be how deep your pockets are to continue. And do you genuinely believe success—real, big, and lasting success—is at the end of this idea rainbow?

26

Celebrate!

A NUMBER OF years ago, we were reading an interview with the late actor/director David Carradine. The article featured a photo of him behind the camera, on the set of the film he was then directing. Taped to the side of the camera was a handwritten note that said, simply and directly, "Share the glory."

Take a deep breath. Exhale. Bring the team together one last time (well, not really—you've got more internal work to do) and make sure everyone is acknowledged. You want to start with the core team, but then work your way out to the organization as a whole.

After thanking your own team, move on to management. Let them know how important their support was in making the project happen. Yes, it's a little suck-up, but so what? Everyone should be feeling expansive at this point, and spreading the glory around certainly can't hurt anyone or his or her career—including the CEO, CFO, CMO, or any other chief. We all appreciate praise, and it's way too often a forgotten component in business.

Strike the right tone, however. Don't be too pompous or too obsequious. Just acknowledge everyone for a job well done. And then move on to the entire company.

Work with your HR people or marketing group—depending on who's in charge of this particular aspect of the company—to develop communications that build awareness throughout the company and acknowledge everyone in the organization for his or her role in helping to make the idea happen.

You'll get two benefits from this. First, everyone in the company will feel more connected to the new process or product. That sense of ownership will make the odds of success that much greater.

Second, it starts to institutionalize the idea of a company Big Idea team. It makes the whole process more real for the organization and that much easier and more desirable for the next team.

So give everyone a pat on the back—then go back to your group and start to put together a manual for the company and for future teams. What did you do well? What did you learn? What were the things you did right? What could you have done better? What were the mistakes you wouldn't make next time? What did you miss that might have made your job easier?

There should have been a note-taker at every meeting. Now's the time to review all the notes and organize them into a complete record of your process and progress. Put together a handbook or write guidelines everyone will be able to refer to during the coming months and years. Make your process a turnkey operation.

Most of all, you want to objectify the win. What's the big picture? Is there something in the new idea—win or lose—that can be applied across your entire company? This is the time to step back and look at the bigger picture.

. . . .
CASE IN POINT

In 1993, ESPN launched ESPN2 as "the deuce"—creating an edgy persona for a network that was going to feature younger and more offbeat sports programming. But by the late 1990s, ESPN2 had lost its distinct visual style and had become a "spillover" network for the mother ship. Ironically, what did them in was their own success! Prior to launching the deuce, ESPN had a typical mainstream sports voice in their announcers, their graphics, and their promo package. But the success of the deuce with younger audiences encouraged ESPN to bring that edgier, more smartass voice over to the main network. Today, everyone thinks of ESPN as being very hip in its programming, graphics, and commercials—mainly because they learned from the baby.
. . . .

Take a page from ESPN and see what you can learn from your newest innovation that can serve your company as a whole.

Finally, we've got to be realistic about the entire process. We said this at the beginning, and we're repeating it now: You might do everything right—and it's still possible that your idea just doesn't launch. Even the great P&G gives up on product ideas that seem like slam-dunks but weren't. So let's talk about the other possibility: failure.

There might come a time when nothing can get the new product/service/idea to launch. Ain't gonna happen. And management is looking at the time and money that's been going into the whole project and finally pulls the plug.

There's an excellent chance someone will paint a big, red target on your back. It would suck if that happened, but let's be real: it does. So, if you absolutely cannot afford to lose your job—say, you have a big mortgage and a growing family—don't take part in the development process. At all. Stay away from the fire because you might get burned.

But even if your attempt is a failure, it doesn't mean you have to fall on your sword. If you've kept management and other divisions informed along the way—if everyone's aware of everything that's been done, if you've kept good notes and can prepare a case study for the organization—there's an excellent chance that senior management will look at this effort as a noble experiment that failed and you'll end up with an A for effort.

We think it's a reasonable risk. And we hope that, when you get to this point in the process, that you're celebrating, not licking your wounds. But as they say, "If someone gives you lemons, make lemonade."

27

The End—And
the Beginning

IN THE 1990S, Steve worked closely with the marketing group of Discovery Communications. He'd travel to Bethesda, Maryland, about two days a week and worked with the creative team in developing promos and marketing materials for their networks. During that time, he saw four different people hired as creative director for the company. And each time, he watched the individual set sail without a compass. Each time, Steve would take the time to sit with the new CD and give him an in-depth briefing of the company: where it was, where it had been, and where it was going. Steve knew it was the smartest way to ensure that he'd continue to be a part of the team—but also a smart way to keep the company on an even keel.

What's next? What's going to happen after your launch is a success?

If your Big Idea becomes a success—big or small—this is the time to make your case for a permanent Big Idea unit in your company. Every business should have one, and the fact that you brought a new idea to marketplace is proof that it works. (But keep in mind that choosing to head a permanent team is a good idea only if you've got complete management buy-in that this process should be a permanent part of the corporate culture.)

The simple truth is that what we've just described is a classic R&D (research & development) unit of a company. If you go back through the annals of corporate history, R&D has always been a part of a good company's business model. What happens, over time, is that the unit either loses its way, loses its focus, or becomes bloated—and then it becomes an easy target for the numbers crunchers to cut.

But these days, R&D serves a whole new purpose. There's just too much new technology being developed and too much opportunity to seize for you not to take advantage of the situation. So more and more companies are committing to advanced or long-range R&D units within or independent of their traditional development functions.

There's an old joke about the five-year-old who goes off to his first day of kindergarten. When he gets home, his mother greets him at the bus and asks him how his day was.

"Great!" the kid enthusiastically responds. "We did building blocks. And played. And had snacks and milk. And had a nap. And played some more. And sang songs. It was terrific!"

"That's wonderful," his mom beams. "Imagine what you're going to do tomorrow."

"Tomorrow?" the kid starts to wail. "I have to go back???"

Yes, you have to go back. You can't let this be a one-time shot. And believe us, there'll be people in the organization who won't want it to continue. Why? Because they'll be jealous. They'll say you were lucky. They'll say you solved the company's competitive problem; now it's time to get back to business as usual. In fact, they'll say all those things we first mentioned in the introduction to this book.

Don't let them win this battle—or the bigger war.

Go and make your case. But don't use the phrase or term "R&D," because it'll be an easy target for your naysayers. Find a name for your band of brothers that will get you the funding to keep it going on a permanent basis. Did someone say BIT—Big Idea Team?

Put everything you learned into a manual. Make it a new part of the corporate culture. If the company's not ready to establish a permanent unit, then encourage people to start their own or embed your process in their daily work and their annual plan. Tell your bosses you're ready to mentor the next group. And when you finally do get that next group, make sure you start them off on the right foot.

For example, ask if you can speak at their first meeting. Let them quiz you on everything you learned—what you did right, what you wished you had done better.

Be gracious. Share it all—good and bad—and encourage them to do even better than you did. You can afford to be magnanimous here—you'll always have the win of having been "the first." But make sure you put something in place so there can be a second, a third Big Idea Team—ad infinitum. So get going:

Don't rest at The Launch. Make sure you get the entire corporate culture thinking Big Idea!

Whether you're an entrepreneur, pro-bono, big business, big brand, SOHO, professional, or a service, make this methodology a regular part of your company's strategy. You really don't have a choice: the marketplace continues to evolve at a pace that demands staying at the leading edge. The relentless pursuit of the Big Idea—large and small—will lead you to innovations and developments that will sustain your company's growth and keep you from becoming extinct.

We'd like to say *Breakthrough!* is a good idea, but the simple truth of this book is that it's a basic necessity.

INDEX

ABOUT THE AUTHORS

This book is a summary of Paul's career. At every step, Big Ideas were the currency of his business practice, and Breakthroughs in the marketplace were the dividends. As president of DDB advertising agency, Griffin Bacal, Paul was one of the inventors of the global smash hit property, Transformers. He was deeply involved with thousands of toys, games, and entertainment properties that have been Breakthroughs around the world.

Prior to Griffin Bacal, Paul honed his approach to innovation at Benton & Bowles and Ogilvy & Mather working for some of the finest marketing organizations in the world: Procter & Gamble, American Express, Kraft/General Foods, and Hasbro. Paul adopted a very simple philosophy: Big Ideas only happen when people believe they are possible, and commit to protecting them every step of the way. In addition to helping invent and steward a range of top new products, services, and brands, Paul has written and spoken extensively about marketing, strategy, and creative innovation at conferences, in print, and on TV and radio interviews.

Paul is also founder of KidShop and Kurnit Communications, and Professor of Marketing and Advertising at Pace University. Throughout his career, Paul has been dedicated to growing businesses through powerful strategic initiatives that have been translated into innovative Big Ideas.

Steve Lance has spent nearly 30 years in advertising and marketing on the creative side of ad agencies and television networks, including creative director of NBC, associate creative director of Backer and Spielvogel, and creative director of the entertainment division of Della Femina, Travisano, and Partners. He's created or been associated with some of the most memorable campaigns in television, including "The More You Know" for NBC and "Shark Week" for the Discovery Channel. He's won numerous creative awards for his campaigns, including Emmy, One Show, Aurora, Mark, and Lifetime Achievement Awards. He's been a member of the board of directors of The Copy Club of New York; a guest lecturer on promotion and advertising at universities, clients, and advertising clubs across America; and he's coauthor of *The Little Blue Book of Advertising* (New York: Penguin/Portfolio, 2006).

Over the years, we've witnessed thousands of ho-hum ideas that have yielded ho-hum results. We're constantly been impressed about the power of Big Ideas and how the same resources put against a Big Idea can drive a Breakthrough.

As seasoned business, marketing, and creative guys, we've been on the inside and the outside of big and small businesses, marketing, creative, and entertainment organizations, and we understand that nothing great gets accomplished without a belief, a method, and a process to make it happen.

In 2007, we founded PS Insights (www.psinsights.com) with our partner, Norman Siegel. PS Insights helps companies of all sizes uncover Big Idea insights about their businesses and the means to bring them to market. We develop speeches, presentations, workshops, training programs, marketing, branded content, and creative solutions for companies who share our vision of Big Idea focus and planning to drive business growth.

We invite you to join the conversation at PSInsights.com or e-mail us:

Paul@psinsights.com

Steve@psinsights.com

You'll also find us on LinkedIn, Facebook, Twitter, Foursquare, and whatever new social networking site that makes sense that hasn't been developed as of this writing.

May 20, 2010